The Shell Book of
S.W. PENINSULA
PATH

Michael Marriott

THE QUEEN ANNE PRESS LIMITED

While the author is here expressing his personal views and opinions, Shell-Mex and B.P. Limited is pleased to be associated with his book.

SBN 362 00066 2

Published by The Queen Anne Press Limited,
49–50 Poland Street, London W.1
and printed in Great Britain by
Purnell and Sons Ltd. Paulton, Nr. Bristol

The South West Peninsula Path, some 515 miles in length, runs westward from Minehead in Somerset, following the North Devon and North Cornish coastline to Land's End, then eastward, following the Channel coast to Studland in Dorset. It is one of the six great footpaths planned in Britain by the Countryside Commission. As yet, there is no right of way over some of the sections, and diversions around these occasional stretches are fully described by the author of this book.

Michael Marriott, experienced both as a pathfinder and camper, has walked extensively in many of the wilder parts of the world, including the Australian bush and Afghanistan. He has also ventured across the Sahara Desert in a taxi! His crisp account of a trek along the Pennine Way, published in this series, established him as one who by means of the written word can communicate the zest and *joie de vivre* that is to be found in the escape from the highroad. He shares with the reader the experience that makes such a walk possible and enjoyable.

"The South West Peninsula Path" is the account of his own experience of that tenuous but fascinating way. His graphic descriptions of the long walk tempt the reader to follow in his footsteps.

CONTENTS

Introduction		7
Foreword		9
1	Preparation	16
2	Somerset: Minehead to County Gate	23
3	North Devon: County Gate to Ilfracombe	28
4	North Devon: Ilfracombe to Cornish Border	33
5	North Cornwall: Marsland Mouth to Newquay	40
6	North Cornwall: Newquay to Land's End	49
7	South Cornwall: Land's End to Falmouth	55
8	South Cornwall: Falmouth to Plymouth	63
9	South Devon: Plymouth to Dartmouth	69
10	South Devon: Dartmouth to Dorset Border	76
11	Dorset: Lyme Regis to Studland and Poole Harbour	82
	Notes on the Plates	90
	Appendices	93

INTRODUCTION

It is a truism that Society only gets what it wants. Thus when Government provides a network of long-distance footpaths and bridleways, it can only be through public demand.

As the population of Britain expands ever more alarmingly and life becomes relentlessly influenced by the pressures of crowding, so the need increases for 'natural breaks'. More and more people simply have to escape our ant-hill connurbations periodically in order to relax, to regain their energy and almost, in many cases, to retain their sanity. Walking, for a growing army of enthusiasts, provides the answer, and it is significant that the pastime is now recognised at the highest levels as an essential part of Britain's outdoor leisure programme. Almost all age groups can participate, very little is required in the way of specialised knowledge or equipment, and the pursuit can be as strenuous or gentle as dictates demand. Nothing is more healthy or invigorating, either physically or mentally. With the inevitable expansion of leisure time, participant sports like walking can only become more popular.

Hence the demand for tracks like the Pennine Way (250 miles), the Pembrokeshire Coast Path (167 miles), Offa's Dyke Path (168 miles) and the South Downs Way (80 miles). Towering above all these is the spectacular South West Peninsula Coast Path, a marathon 515 miles which will be the longest unbroken path in the country when officially completed. It is this magnificent Way that is the subject of this guide.

An exciting, challenging route that the reader can tackle in its entirety or piece-meal with the aid of his car. Certainly the latter method will be far and away the most popular, but whether walking the whole length or merely a few miles, this first-ever guide will prove an essentially practical companion.

It will help the walker, novice and experienced, to enjoy some of the loveliest countryside in these islands of ours, covering four counties along a path that in all its length rarely strays more than the proverbial stone's throw from the sea.

Just to clarify the description long-distance footpath, we quote the Countryside Commission.

"Long-distance footpaths (or bridleways) are national routes with continuous rights of way offering facilities for extensive journeys which, for the most part, avoid roads used by motor traffic."

So far as the Peninsula Path is concerned, at the time of writing there are still a number of stretches where no rights of way exist, and therefore care must be taken to avoid trespass. Every such section is clearly marked in the accompanying maps and described in the text, including detours for both walkers and drivers.

It will be appreciated that the completion of any long-distance footpath involves a great deal of negotiating with private owners and it is often a very protracted business. It took thirty years of stubborn battling before the Pennine Way, for example, was opened officially in 1965. The inspiration of Tom Stephenson, later Secretary of the Ramblers' Association, the Pennine Way was taken up by the National Parks Commission who were given statutory powers to establish long-distance footpaths and bridleways. The Countryside Commission is now responsible for this network of wanderways, routed in conjunction with county and local authorities, for those eager to explore on foot. Whilst the Peninsula Path is still officially incomplete, the restricted stretches are relatively few and far between (especially when the total mileage is considered), and offer no real deterrent to the enthusiast who wishes to walk it fully or in part, here and now . . .

FOREWORD

Much of the fascination of the four counties through which the Peninsula Path passes lies in their distinctive individuality. Each is quite different from the others and even within boundary confines there are frequently marked contrasts of landscape, architecture and climate. Each county even has its own edible trade-mark, and no visit would be complete without the sampling of Somerset cider, Dorset knobs, Devon cream and Cornish pasties.

Somerset

The Somerset stretch of the path is comparatively short, but within its length it encompasses some of the finest scenery in Great Britain. Porlock Hill, for example, must be familiar to millions of drivers, but only a fraction of the surrounding beauty can be seen from a car. Far better to park, get out and walk, so as to enjoy a really memorable visit to the area.

Somerset, in fact, is a holiday county par excellence for the walker, for there are many open areas like Exmoor, the Quantocks and the Mendips, together with a whole network of way-marked footpaths to explore, quite apart from the Peninsula Path.

The county covers an area of some 1630 square miles and contains celebrated gems like Cheddar Gorge, a narrow defile which winds for two miles between soaring limestone crags. In the village they specialise in the world-famous cheese, and there are the giant stalactites in the nearby caves. Then there is Wookey Hole, the magnificent cathedral city of Wells and the beaches so beloved by the family holiday-maker around Weston-super-Mare.

West of Sedgemoor, the great region of hills extends from Devon to the sea. These consist of the Black Down, Brendon and Quantock Hills, with Exmoor dominating the western side. This entire district is renowned for its grandeur; a place of wild, even desolate moorland, the bold outlines and height of its hills culminating with Dunkery Beacon at 1707 feet above sea level.

The two principal rivers of the county are the Avon and Parrett, while the Exe is much favoured by trout fishermen. Essentially agricultural, some four-fifths of Somerset are under cultivation, though most of this productive ground is in the flatter, river valley areas inland from the rugged north-western coastline.

Bath, Glastonbury and Dunster are just three of Somerset's historic delights, and Taunton, the fine county town, was the scene of the infamous Bloody Assizes held by Judge Jeffreys after the Monmouth Rebellion. The castle here contains a very interesting museum and is well worth a visit. As for the coastal path, which we are about to study in detail, this provides excellent walking over well defined paths and is always amid lovely surroundings.

Devonshire

Devonshire, covering an area of 2604 square miles, is the third largest county in England, exceeded in size only by Yorkshire and Lincolnshire. Nearly the whole land mass, unlike Somerset which possesses a lot of lowland, is broken and hilly. It is also the highest land area in England, south of Derbyshire and the Welsh border.

The scenery, it need hardly be said, is much varied and in parts breathtaking in its beauty. The uplands of Exmoor, as they lead from Somerset, are still the haunt of wild red deer and the hardy little ponies which take their name from the area.

Dartmoor, the dominating physical feature of Devonshire, is world renowned for its stark, alluring contours and its old penal centre at Princetown. Though those who intend following the coastal path will catch nothing more than a glimpse or two of the fringes near Plymouth, it is always there, brooding yet inviting for those who like exploring the wilder areas of our countryside.

Features which are unmistakably Devonian are the cosy thatched cottages and the deep hedged roads and lanes sunk below the common level of the ground. This kind of hedging can often be irritating to the motorist, who could traverse the whole county by minor roads and barely see anything but a close-up of foliage. All the more reason then to leave the driving seat and explore on foot.

The north and south coasts differ markedly in character, as you will see, but both have grand cliff and rock scenery, unsurpassed by any in England or Wales – in some ways resembling the Mediterranean seaboard in its range of colour.

The long combes down which the rivers flow are densely wooded, and the county immediately inland is invariably of great natural beauty. The Tamar, Teign, Dart, Exe, Plym, Tavy, Taw and Torridge literally network the county, and each and every one is a delight to the eye, winding down from the heights to the Atlantic or the English Channel. Devon is a place of rivers and streams and you can't wander far along any of its countless footpaths without coming across some tinkling water, gin clear and providing a home for a whole wealth of wild life.

The climate varies greatly, with semi-tropical plant life thriving on the southern coastline and the ruggedness of Dartmoor, inland, where the air is sharp and bracing and the snow lies long in winter.

Essentially agricultural, modern Devon nevertheless relies heavily on tourism. Dairy farming is the mainstay of the economy, however, supported by a certain amount of quarrying, and much governmental industry around Plymouth and Devonport. The cathedral city of Exeter is the county town and has, of course, been of strategic importance since Roman times. Today it is probably more renowned among holiday drivers as a notorious bottleneck. Be that as it may, Exeter is a magnificent West Country city, with fine shopping centres, Tudor and Stuart houses and Georgian crescents. Cathedral Square is particularly enchanting.

The distinctive red earth of Devon has seen the birth of many famous British seafarers, and one could hardly mention the county without thinking almost automatically of Drake and Raleigh. The whole coastline is punctuated with illustrious history and the Peninsula Path passes through or near all the ports and havens that make up much of our maritime past.

Cornwall

The south-westernmost county of England rightly lays claim to being the most individual in the land. No area possesses a stronger character than Cornwall, which is in many ways unique. Its economic and social conditions, its history and traditions are all distinctly different, and even the physical characteristics of the terrain are unmatched. This great rugged promontory is some 75 miles in length and has an extreme breadth of some 45 miles where it joins the Devonshire border. The county actually covers some 1350 square miles, with the River Tamar forming much of the boundary line with Devon.

To the west of Launceston the mass of high ground rises to 1375 feet, the summit of Brown Willy. This district is broken and wild, with rough tors and boulder-strewn plateaux, and although little can be seen from the coast path, Bodmin Moor always makes a fascinating inland detour.

There is similar high country inland from St Austell, between Helston and Redruth and north-west from Penzance. The true Cornish hinterland is bare and desolate and heavily scarred by old mine workings. There is very little agriculture in the uplands, most of the county's natural wealth lying beneath the earth, and there is no question that much of inland Cornwall is stern and unpretty. Harsh and sparse, it holds limited appeal for the average holiday visitor, whether he is in the car or on foot.

Those who trace the coastal path will undoubtedly see the best of the county, for it is the great combes and valleys that descend from the upper moorland to the coast, on both sides, that make up the wealth of scenic beauty. These valleys are frequently well wooded and, in the luxuriance of their vegetation, strongly characteristic.

The small rivers traversing the combes often enter fine

estuaries which penetrate deeply into the land. On the south coast the great inlets of the Tamar – which divides Cornwall from Devon – and the Looe and Fowey Rivers are typical examples. Falmouth Harbour is the most important of the purely Cornish inlets and is accessible to the largest sea-going vessels. Helford River is another waterway of striking grandeur, much beloved by small boat enthusiasts.

In the north, the estuaries of the Camel and the Hayle spill respectively into Padstow Bay and St Ives Bay. Save for such inlets, the whole coast is almost totally rock-bound and the cliff panorama is quite unsurpassed in England for its sheer rugged splendour. On the north coast, from Tintagel Head and Boscastle northwards to Hartland Point in Devon, the dark slate cliffs with their narrow and distorted strata are remarkably rugged of outline owing to the continual onslaught of the Atlantic surf.

Southwards, in the splendid little bays and inlets in the neighbourhood of the Lizard, the serpentine rock is singular for its exquisite colouring, and the rock faces around Land's End are splendid granite barriers of regal majesty. The Peninsula Path, of course, traces its way across all the subtle changes in the coastal strata, providing an ever-changing vista for the walker and driver alike.

Even the climate of Cornwall has a character of its own. Snow seldom lies for more than a few days and the winters are less severe than in any other part of the country. The near-constant sea winds prevent trees attaining any great size, except in a few sheltered places, but the air is mild and the lower vegetation, especially around Penzance, is almost subtropical in its lushness. There is a strong love of home country among the Cornish people, who are very independent and proud of their Celtic ancestry. Like the Welsh, they can be great orators and are a sturdy race well suited to the rugged, sea-girt terrain.

Finally there is the Cornwall of Legend. All over the county there are relics of prehistoric man, burial mounds, circles and huts. From such prehistoric remains do myths and legends thrive, and from the mists of time there survives to this day a mystique of pixies, ghosts, and shadowy heroes like King

Arthur. Admittedly, much of this folk-lore is kept alive in the name of tourism, but for all that there are many secret and unfrequented places in Cornwall where the stranger feels an eeriness and a distinct tug of the primeval. Bodmin Moor in a storm is one such place and the lonely, wild stretches of the Atlantic coastline provide others. Even today, the visitor feels somehow that this "Last County" is a totally separate part of England, stern, remote and indifferent to the march of progress. That this atmosphere adds greatly to a walking and driving tour of the county is unquestionable.

Dorset

Dorsetshire is one of the loveliest counties in all Britain though, curiously, relatively few of the annual flood of car-borne visitors to the West Country are aware of its hidden beauty, for little is seen from the main through-route trunk roads. Dorset is apparently considered a transit county, en-route to the seemingly more romantic Devon and Cornwall. This is a great pity, for within its boundaries Dorset has a coastline as majestic as any further west; a history which has had a profound effect on this country as a whole; some riveting relics, like Corfe Castle, and – of increasing importance in an era of road crowding – space to move about at leisure even in the height of the summer season. Nearly every township in the county can trace its history back beyond William the Conqueror, with Wareham, Shaftesbury and Dorchester itself being rich in the relics of antiquity. The Purbeck Hills, Lulworth Cove, the Kimmeridge Ledges and St Alban's Head are all splendid high spots and they are all on the route of the coastal path.

The Dorset section of the Peninsula Path is, in fact, a sheer delight to walk. The Hardy Country has, in essence, changed little since that literary giant used the area as such a graphic setting for his novels.

Smallest of the four counties, Dorset covers an area of some 990 square miles and its terrain is for the most part broken and hilly. The principal river is the Stour, which rises just over the Wiltshire border and flows in a south-easterly course to join the Hampshire Avon close to its mouth. Among the Dorset high spots in an essentially pastoral county, are the broad line of hills which run from east to west, inland from Dorchester and Blandford Forum; the scenically exciting Purbeck Hills with their world-famous stone and marble; the strange formation of Chesil Bank; and one of the finest natural harbours in the world at Poole. The impressive Portland Bill, four miles south of Weymouth, is a limestone island joined by the pebbly ridge of Chesil Bank. From its stone was built St Paul's Cathedral, parts of the Houses of Parliament and countless other buildings up and down the land. Swanage and Studland Bay provide a suitably scenic finish to the Peninsula Path.

Like so much of the country we are about to explore, the air of Dorest is gratifyingly mild and in some of the more sheltered spots on the coast there is a fair share of sub-tropical growth. Not generally well wooded (despite the lushness of the Vale of Blackmore), Dorset is a rolling, open land of heath and wide skies, with many splendid back lanes and some extremely attractive villages. It is a county with great appeal to those who like to see England in a leisurely manner, preferably on their own two feet.

The West Country, as a whole then, might have been made expressly for the tourist. Not without reason is it the most popular of all holiday areas in Great Britain, and it is now beginning to attract an increasing flow of foreign visitors.

1   PREPARATION

The South West Peninsula Coast Path begins at Minehead in Somerset and runs along the Somerset, North Devon, North and South Cornwall, South Devon and Dorset coastlines. With a number of short breaks, where sections of the route are still under negotiation, it finishes at Studland, near Swanage, in Dorset.

Unquestionably the longest continuous footpath in the country – and likely to remain so for many years – the Peninsula Path also has the distinction of being the most "civilised". The majority of long-distance paths run through the wilder places of Britain, usually over moorland, through forests, across the tops of hills and mountains. This is both logical and highly desirable, and the veteran walker would have them no different. Indeed, their main attractions include the promise of near solitude, a chance to see wild life as it should be seen, and a dearth of man-made landmarks.

With the Peninsula Path, however, the major consideration (quite rightly) has been to follow the coastline as closely as possible for its entire length. To do this in four leading holiday counties (two of which share the distinction of being the most popular in the whole country) means that areas of real wilderness will be relatively rare. Which in turn can only be considered an advantage for the novice family walker who wants to get away from his car periodically but who is perhaps wary of the sterner stuff of high-level walking.

Not that the Peninsula Path should in any way be underestimated. There are some really rugged sections, particularly in North Cornwall, that would (and do) put the toughest walker to the test. Nonetheless, for the most part there is the constant comfort to the newcomer that navigation need only be rudimentary, for with the sea so near he can hardly go astray. And whilst the path winds across the tops of many cliffs, the route could never be described as "high-level"; there are none of the hazards of rapid weather deterioration that the more remote paths incur.

So, rugged in parts, threading its way around some of the most romantic coastlines in the country, the Peninsula Path is an eminently safe route, ideally suitable as a challenging adventure for the whole family, even if their only previous experience of walking be nominal. In short, this Path presents a really exciting prospect to the man ready and willing to shut the car door behind him with more frequency on his next visit to the West Country.

Clothing and Equipment.

There is no reason why short stretches of the path shouldn't be walked in lounge suits or party dresses, as a leg-stretching exercise to combat car-cramp. Indeed, for many people on holiday, walking *is* an impulse activity – never more than a short stroll along an inviting path, never further than a horn-blast from the waiting car. Those who are lured onwards, ill-dressed and ill-equipped, are frequently the ones who have to be rescued, suffering from turned ankles, exposure and fright. Even the gentlest English countryside can be very stern with those who would treat her lightly. Especially those citizens more used to concrete and neon surroundings.

However, if you are reading this guide, you must be considering more than the odd stroll and it is hoped that the following chapters will tempt you to something more ambitious. Call it serious walking if you will; at least it will be a deliberate, planned pursuit rather than a series of impromptu ambles.

What then *is* a serious walk? Much depends on age, condition, aptitude and enthusiasm. The hardened fell-walker will think nothing of completing 25 to 30 miles in a day, often over extremely rugged terrain. Conversely, for the man or woman in middle years, to whom walking is a new game, six miles in the same time might well be a commendable achievement. This really is the secret of enjoyment in walking. Do no more than you can comfortably achieve, and, in the initial stages at least, count the *time* you spend on your two feet, rather than the miles. Set yourself a target well within capability and if you happen to exceed it, then the feeling of well-being at the end of the day will be even more marked.

The most important contributive factor to efficient and comfortable walking is, of course, footwear. People walk over every type of terrain in anything from sneakers to dancing shoes! It can be done, but there is no question at all that correct footwear is far and away the best and the safest. Walking boots with built-in ankle supports, non-slip "Commando" soles, and double-tongued to provide total waterproofing are really essential. If for any reason you simply cannot wear boots, then go for a stout walking shoe, again with non-slip soles. A comprehensive selection will be found in any good outdoor-life stores.

Always wear such boots with at least two pairs of socks, the outer pair being of the thick oiled-wool type. It is imperative that any new pair of boots or shoes be tried on in the shop with the socks you intend wearing, to ensure that you buy the correct size – as a rule, one larger than usual.

Almost equally important is the way you break-in the new boots. Buy them well before any intended holiday walking and wear them around the house, in the garden and for short strolls, so they mould gradually to your foot without causing blisters. Assist this process by coating them liberally with dubbin two or three times during the first few weeks. After this, dubbin them only occasionally, say three or four times a year. Too much lubrication will affect the stitching, which will then "work" and ruin the proofing. Good boots are not cheap, (no craftsman-made product can be) and you will have to pay from £8 to £10. Take care of them though, and they will last indefinitely. There is the whole world of difference between walking in town shoes and in pukka walking boots cushioned with two or three pairs of socks.

The anorak is now the standard over-garment for most outdoor pursuits, and really it has no peers. We refer, of course, to the orthodox anorak made of close-weave cotton, possibly double lined, with no zips or buttons in the front to allow wind penetration, a generous hood, draw-strings at neck and waist and a crutch strap. The anorak is not waterproof, but it does "breathe", which helps to dissipate perspiration in a way that no artificial material can. In any case the pocket nylon cape or mac is more or less essential, so proofing is not all that important. It is the wind-resistance and freedom of movement that the garment provides that is so important. Again, generosity of cut is vital so that a couple of pullovers may be worn beneath, if necessary, without restricting movement. The cost will be from £4 to £10 according to cut and quality.

For lower limb protection, slacks of thorn-proof or cavalry twill material are favourite with both sexes, though climbing trousers are currently enjoying a boom with walkers. These have the advantage of terminating just below the knee, so that you can cover calves with over-socks or leave them bare in hot weather. Shorts are not recommended, particularly for the Peninsula Path, which has its share of brambles and wind-swept headlands. In any case you can always cool off, whilst it is not so easy to get warm once a chill wind has stiffened all your leg muscles.

So much then for the main items of clothing. What you wear underneath is largely a matter of choice, but remember that two thin pullovers will be warmer than one thick one and that you can thus shed or don by degrees according to conditions.

The walker is singularly blessed, for of all outdoor sports and pastimes, his equipment list is the shortest. You will need a small haversack to carry the few necessities though, and once again this should be selected carefully. No matter how light your load, it must be carried properly for continuous comfort. That is, in the centre of your back, supported by two shoulder straps. The single strap haversack or draw-string duffle-bag is not suitable, as you will discover after the first mile or so.

The bag should be strongly made, reasonably waterproof, and whilst capable of carrying your needs, should not be too big. The temptation to fill it, whatever the size, will be difficult to resist.

Inside you should carry the following items: spare pullover, lightweight rainwear, a bar of Kendal Mint Cake or other emergency food ration, a whistle and small torch (just in case you get lost or become injured), a compass and (most important) a set of one-inch Ordnance Survey maps of the area you intend to tackle. Unless you plan to stop at inns or cafes for refreshment, you will also need to allow for sandwiches, and there will probably be personal items like camera or binoculars. Use one of the rucksack pockets for all your pocket items too, like keys, wallet, spare coins and so on. The emptier your pockets, the easier your walking will be. Drink has deliberately been omitted, for it is heavy and (on most stretches of the Peninsula Path) a needless burden, as you will see.

So much for equipment—though you might like to bear in mind that a stout walking stick makes a good companion over rough country; a well-trained dog makes a better one, and the two together are ideal.

You Need a Compass

Finally, there is the business of navigation which, though not so vital as with other long-distance paths, is still important. Certain parts of the Peninsular coastline, especially the Cornish sector, are subject to heavy sea mists at times and these can roll in very quickly under certain conditions. They are not serious hazards provided you know for *certain* in which direction you are walking, and this is only possible if you have a compass and know how to read it. This little instrument is cheap but indispensible. Quite apart from being an emergency device to get you back to civilisation quickly, it also provides a vital link between map and field, ensuring that you never have to make long, exhausting detours because of route uncertainty.

Quite as important as the compass (more so in some ways), are the Ordnance Survey maps. These really are the most illuminating guides to those familiar with the series . . . easy to read and understand, and pin-pointing with great accuracy any feature of note in the area of landscape covered. For the Peninsula Path the One Inch Series is advocated and you will need the following set to cover the Minehead to Land's End route; Sheets No. 163, 164, 174, 185, 189. From Land's End to Studland, sheets No. 189, 190, 186, 188, 176, 177, 178, 179.

In this guide mention is made of car-parking locations and overnight accommodation of all kinds where considered necessary, together with details of local bus services. Thus, if there is a particular stretch that holds special appeal you can tackle it as a separate project with a definite start and finish. Consequently, no matter where you happen to be touring, within striking distance of the Peninsula Coast that is, there will be walks of varying distances near to hand, together with mileages to assist selection, and a bus not too far distant to carry you back to the car.

One final word on preliminaries. Don't expect any long-distance footpath to look like a motor road in miniature. Ofttimes you will have to indulge in a certain amount of detective work to select the correct path from local networks, and to rediscover it where breaks for towns and resorts occur. Moreover, a single glance at any contour map of the West Country coastline will show that undulations are the rule rather than the exception. Gates and styles are too numerous to mention, whilst signposting is, at the time of writing, sporadic. No doubt within the next few years this last-mentioned will be improved and, in fact, the Countryside Commission have designed an intriguing and distinctive little acorn sign which will increasingly be used to mark stretches of all long-distance footpaths. But basically there will be few "improvements" to the Peninsula Path. Rightly so, for there has to be an element of challenge in any worthwhile footpath, which must, so far as possible, be left in a totally natural state.

So much, then, for preparation. Now, without further ado, let's begin the long walk.

THE ROUTE FROM MINEHEAD TO LAND'S END

This first section of the Peninsula path offers a variety of fine scenery to the walker. The Somerset route includes an exhilarating stretch over the heights of Exmoor, whilst in Devon the beauty of Lynmouth and the remainder of the coast to Hartland Point is familiar to many. South of Hartland Point the coast is equally beautiful and those who are familiar with the high wild coastline to the north of Bude will find similar characteristics in the cliffs hereabouts.

The North Cornwall route enables the walker to appreciate

to the full the essential beauty of the county, with its long stretches of magnificent cliffs and headlands, fine beaches and picturesque little harbours and fishing villages. The path follows the cliff tops as closely as possible and makes little use of cultivated land.

THE ROUTE FROM LAND'S END TO STUDLAND

The Cornish south coast path follows the cliff edges as nearly as possible, taking the walker through magnificent coastal scenery and a number of attractive fishing villages. Many places of historical interest are also within easy reach.

The geological structure of south Devon is complex and there is a fascinating variety of scene on this essentially coastal path of some 93 miles. This takes in the estuaries of the Yealm, the Erme and the Avon in the west, the curious stretch north from Torcross alongside Slapton Ley, the magnificent Dart Estuary, the great limestone promontory of Bovey Head, the sweep of Torbay succeeded by the red cliffs from Babbacombe. And then, beyond the Exe, lie the fine chalk cliffs round Beer and the landslip east of Seaton.

The Dorset coastal path, roughly 72 miles long, traverses a variety of scenery comprising cliff, downland, shingle and sand-dune. At West Bexington and Osmington Mills the walker is given a choice of two routes. Some of the finest walking in Britain is to be found between Lyme Regis and Swanage.

2   SOMERSET: MINEHEAD
TO COUNTY GATE

The Peninsula Path begins, not spectacularly, but rather
casually, winding upwards from the end of Minehead Quay.
There is nothing, as yet, to denote the great adventure ahead,
merely a signpost stating baldly, "Cliff Path to Greenaleigh
Farm". A wooded ascent, pleasant enough once the municipal
tipping ground on the seaward side has been left behind and
below. But before striding out on this, the first leg of the
journey, what has Minehead to offer as a home-base for the
walker who also happens to be a car owner?

To begin with, the distance from London is a convenient
170 miles (even less from Birmingham), enough to make for
a day's interesting driving without being exhausting. As those
familiar with this popular area of the West Country will
already know, Minehead is an interesting mixture of ancient
and modern.

On the one hand there are tree-lined avenues, excellent
shopping facilities, formal gardens, plenty of evening entertainment and a large open-air swimming pool. There is also
a wealth of golf, tennis, fishing, coach excursions and steamer
trips. More important, perhaps, there is every kind of accommodation both within the town environs and in the outskirt
villages. Touring pitches, for those with independent units, are
somewhat limited, although there are one or two excellent
caravan and camping sites between Minehead and Lynmouth,
the next township along the footpath. Good car-parking is
available, some of it free, but be prepared for difficulties in this
direction during July and August.

For those who prefer the not-so-new, Old Minehead has a
16th-century jetty, fishermen's chapel and a splendid hillside
church reached by steps which climb between a cluster of

thatched and lime-washed cottages. Fine sandy beaches too, though the tide recedes a very long way. Market Day is every third Monday in the month; early closing each Wednesday.

Make your way to the Quay then, and to the end of the road between the coastguard station and harbour. If the time of the year is right (and this really means any month outside July and August), you should be able to park the car easily hereabouts.

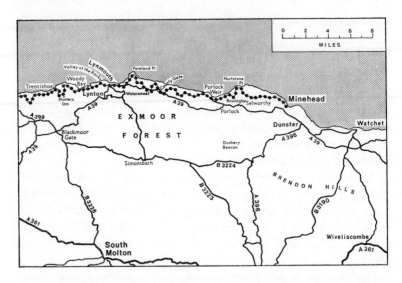

The ascent westwards is fairly steep at first, through Culver Cliff Wood, a wide stony track also frequently used by horse-riders. Keep your eye on the wide horizon seaward and you'll hardly notice the tip area below. In one mile there is a fork path coastwards, to an old smuggler's cave and a ruined chapel. The main track, however, maintains a south-western direction and levels out to traverse North Hill.

This is a superb table-land, roughly three miles of high level walking along a metalled road to Selworthy Beacon. But it is an unfenced road, and does not normally carry a lot of traffic, for it is a one-way route to the Beacon viewpoint at an elevation of 1013 feet. You can walk along the verge, or use any of the sheep tracks or alternative paths in the vicinity so long as they continue generally south-westwards.

If you are out of practice, these four miles may be enough for the first day. In this case, if someone in your party is willing to collect you with the car, this is the way for him to get to the Beacon by road. Head for Blenheim Road in the centre of Minehead and take the steep hill adjacent to the Plume of Feathers Hotel. Pass the war memorial and then follow the signposts to North Hill. As mentioned, the road ends at the Beacon.

For the more energetic, the path continues and descends via Bossington Hill and Hurtstone Combe. Another fork, approximately one mile from the Beacon, leads to Hurtstone Point; this path rejoins the main route again, so keep to the inland track if you wish to cut out the Point detour. There is a short length of metalled road through Bossington and then, on reaching sea level, the path follows Bossington and Porlock beaches, thankfully above the pebble line, to rejoin the road (via steps up from the beach) a short distance from Porlock Weir.

Porlock Weir, 4½ miles from Selworthy Beacon, is a charming little cluster of cottages around a most scenic walled small-boat harbour, with a mellowed inn and one or two little shops. There is good car-park here and for 1s. 6d. per day you can come and go as you please; an excellent base from which to explore the coastal path in this region. There is a branch path here to the remains of an old manor near Gore Point.

The main path bears due west, and a further short stretch of tarmac will indicate the correct route after leaving the Weir. Splendid country now as the path begins its gradual ascent alongside Yearnor Wood to continue high above the sea. In 1¾ miles you reach Culbone. Stop a while here, for this tiny church, far from any road, is the smallest in all England. Just under one mile further and you come to Silcombe, just a couple of farms and the start of another lane. Don't worry though, this is very much single track, with grass sprouting from the centre, and it only continues for about 1½ miles.

Broomstreet is at the end of this section with Yenworthy following about a mile later. The path crosses the A39 at County Gate, the Somerset/Devon border. The approximate distance from Porlock Weir to this point is 4¾ miles. Another excellent free car park, with toilets thoughtfully provided by the Devon County Council, offers a strategic pick-up point or day-parking area. A most pleasant 3 mile stroll can be taken from here back to Culbone and that minuscule church, along a well defined and fairly level path.

This, then, is the first lap, a total footpath distance of roughly 13½ miles, taking in one of the scenic prides of Somerset. The whole length runs roughly parallel to the main A39 trunk road, so if you happen to be caught in a mist or become uncertain of your direction, simply walk due south. Porlock and its famous hill (1 in 4 in places), is a good halfway house as it were, but you will have to walk back from Porlock Weir through West Porlock.

Another good drive-and-walk route is that via Porlock Toll Road. The charge for the car is 2s., but this is well worth while for the scenic downhill drive. Indeed, this road is most pleasant to walk down in early Spring or late Autumn, and you can always leave the car safely at the top. Touring accommodation will be found at Porlock Caravan Park, just off the main street, and it is nearly always possible to hire a caravan for a few days at a modest fee outside the high season. Another recommended site is Burrowhayes Farm, West Luccombe, about 2 miles south-east of Porlock. A lovely setting, this, on the fringe of Exmoor, with static caravans for hire and room for tourers and tenters. Both sites are open from Easter to October. Bed and Breakfast facilities and hotel accommodation are so numerous around here there is no point in listing them.

Dunkery Beacon

There are, incidentally, several scenic high spots which must be mentioned, all within easy reach of this first footpath section. Dunkery Beacon, the highest point on Exmoor (1,707 feet), roughly 4 miles south of Porlock, gives superb panoramic views not only of the wild Exmoor beauty, but also, on a clear day, across the Bristol Channel and into Wales. Dunster, 2¼ miles south-east of Minehead, is a delightful village dominated by a fine old castle. A quaint medieval Yarn Market stands in the centre of the broad main street (a great attraction to photographers), and the historic church and huge dovecot are key tourist attractions. If time permits, try also to see the little hamlet of Selworthy, with its venerable church and cottages clinging to the hillside.

Whether or not you have the time and the inclination to make such side excursions, either on foot or by car, you will certainly feel the benefit if you walk the footpath route. In the right seasonal conditions you will meet few other people between Minehead and County Gate, and those you do see will be in sympathy with your mood – which will assuredly be one of benign contentment. This fringe of Exmoor provides a chance to feast the eyes on distant horizons of splendid combes and rolling heather-clad uplands; a tonic for those of us who spend most of our lives looking at close-ups of concrete and tarmac. And this is part of the object of this guide; to offer a brief escape to natural country and a slow re-discovery of the pleasure of using legs as nature intended.

An annual holiday spent following, either partly or wholly, the rest of the Peninsula Path as it unfolds in the coming chapters, will engender a feeling of well-being which will never be captured by sitting behind the steering wheel or lazing on the beach.

3   NORTH DEVON:
COUNTY GATE TO ILFRACOMBE

Sadly and all too often, the traveller, whether on foot or in a car, crosses a county boundary in Britain and is virtually unaware that he has done so. It is true, that in latter years local authorities have marked boundary lines more diligently, but many are still barely noticeable. Not so with the Somerset/ Devon dividing line. County Gate is a very distinctive landmark where even the terrain seems to change subtly as if to announce to each and every new arrival that here is the County of Devonshire. There is nothing really spectacular about the old stone gate house and the adjacent car park on the Devon side, save that in its isolation high above the sea, with no other habitation immediately in sight, it has the air and character of a sentinel.

At this point one crosses the main A39 trunk road, which will certainly be carrying waves of heavy traffic during the high season, and great care is needed. The path is very clearly defined, ascending Cosgate Hill, an area of Open Access land, and then descending to rejoin the main road. The next section is not yet available, and the walker is therefore forced to use the narrow verge alongside the road for three-quarters of a mile. Care is needed, especially if children are in the party, though by now most cars are reducing speed drastically, as this is the summit region. You switch from one side of the road to the other during this stretch, the western half of which runs along a raised verge on the southern side of the road; the latter is not yet a legal right of way, but the landowner is not likely to object to genuine walkers.

After this roadside stretch, the path veers seaward in a north-westerly direction, to skirt Kipscombe Hill and cross the two miles or so of Countisbury Common. This is a magnificent area of country, with a couple of fork paths out to Foreland Point Lighthouse. The cliff path from Countisbury hamlet to the lighthouse (for those wishing to make the detour) should be negotiated with care. A picturesque inn and small camping field will be found at Countisbury, for those interested, but a short detour is necessary south from the footpath to reach them. The main path continues for half a mile, then recrosses the A39 once more to follow the very steep motor road adjacent to Wind Hill. Holding mainly to the southern side of the road, it sweeps down into the film-set harbour and village of Lynmouth.

Lynmouth and its high-level twin resort of Lynton, constitute one of the undisputed high spots of the whole Peninsula Path. One could spend the whole of any annual holiday exploring the profusion of cliff walks which have been so efficiently way-marked in this area. There is a large car-park adjacent to the harbour and every conceivable type of accommodation, together with a particularly good touring ground halfway between the twin townships at Lynbridge, called Sunny Lyn Caravan and Camping Site.

This area, as almost everyone knows, is Devon at its best, whilst both Lynton and Lynmouth are the recognised holiday centres of Exmoor National Park. Lynmouth and its bijou harbour lies at the mouth of the River Lyn. Lynton is perched 500 feet above and nestles amid luxuriant wooded cliffs. The two are connected by a quaint and exceedingly steep cliff railway. Market Day is on Saturday and early closing is Thursday. Whilst this guide is expressly concerned with the Peninsula Path, mention must be made of two absolutely delightful walks hereabouts, which make a brief stay in Lynmouth very worth while. The first is alongside the East Lyn, through the wooded gorge to Watersmeet where, as the name implies, two rivers meet in a flurry of waterfalls and shallow rapids under a timber bridge. An easy footpath all the way, about $2\frac{3}{4}$ miles in length, with a tea garden at the end, provides an enchanting stroll. The second runs from the Sunny Lyn Caravan and Camping Site, over the pack-horse bridge by the little inn, and onwards and upward through wooded slopes to The Cleave. Superb, near-aerial views appear over Lynton and Lynmouth as you top Summerhouse Hill. The distance to Watersmeet via this route is again 2¾ miles.

Whilst staying in the vicinity it is essential to see Lynmouth after dark, preferably at high water; a beautiful harbour is Lynmouth, if ever there was one, with small boats dancing on the water and reflecting the fairy lights strung in profusion along the waterfront. Very steep hills abound whichever direction you take in the car, but there are plenty of escape roads and frequent dire warnings about engaging low gear. An efficient service and repair garage is found conveniently close to the municipal car park in Lynmouth.

The coastal path breaks here, as it does through all the major towns and villages along the route, and you pick it up again just north-west of Lynton, where it winds over Hollerday Hill (signposted), and on through the spectacular Valley of Rocks—a huge natural arena formed between fern-clad hills to the south and grotesque rock peaks on the seaward side. This is a superb stretch and if you have left the car in Lynton itself (probably at the spacious municipal park) a most exhilarating start to the next stage.

As an alternative you can leave the car actually in the Valley of Rocks, by simply following the sign-posting from the village. A spacious attended car park is provided and there is a refreshment hut open during the summer season. The path now hugs a narrow toll road for just over 2 miles. You can walk on the road or along the verges, which is much more pleasant, but you can't escape the road altogether owing to the cliff formation, which is decidedly sheer in parts. Fine, open scenery at first and then into the trees and on to the aptly-named Woody Bay. If you fancy a swim there is access to the beach (with limited car parking for those behind the wheel), nearby to the toll house. Motorists pay 1s., but walkers have free access.

Keep to the single track road from this point and, at the junction, take the Woody Bay Hotel fork which is signposted, and not the road to Parracombe. This is a most pleasant road to walk on, traversing thickly wooded slopes with bird's-eye peeps of the foreshore through gaps in the trees. Better to keep to the metalled road, rather than take the old cliff footpath which is now considered unsafe.

In a short distance you will pass a turn-off to Martinhoe Mansion. Continue on and in three-quarters of a mile, at the hairpin bend, there is the gateway to the Old Coach Road. This is now a green track and gives easy walking over a well-graded surface. It's not difficult to let your imagination wander here, to conjure the clip-clop of the coach and four, stove-pipe hats and rustling crinolines.

Now follows yet another fine section of the Path, which winds seawards around The Beacon, roughly 1½ miles from the Toll House. In another 1¼ miles you drop down into a steep and most beautiful combe to reach the well-known Hunter's Inn, near the mouth of the picturesque River Heddon. Along this stretch you will be able to spot the old, lower path quite easily. Keep to the higher elevation though to avoid the danger spots near the cliff edges. Another half-mile of tarmac lane constitutes the official route.

From here one follows a rather tricky section of the path comprising the 5¾ miles westwards from Hunter's Inn to Combe Martin. Although much of it is not yet an official right of way, there are good lengths available to walkers, either over the extensive National Trust property at the western end or along the Hangman Walk near Combe Martin.

Nonetheless, at the time of writing there are one or two private stretches which must be respected. Therefore it will probably be advantageous to follow the little minor road from Hunter's Inn, through the hamlet of Trentishoe and continue due west. Very quickly you break into high level open country, where the road is unfenced and where the verges are ready made for the walker. There are two car parks approximately one mile south-west of Trentishoe.

Continue on this road until you pass a footpath signpost to Holdstone Hill. Pass this and a little further along will be seen a second signpost showing Combe Martin to be 2¼ miles distant. Take this track, which leads up and over Knap Down, past Great and Little Hangman and thence, via any one of three tracks, to the pictorial descent into Combe Martin. The path emerges at the municipal car park, where a mobile

Exmoor National Park Information Centre operates throughout the Summer season.

Combe Martin must have one of the longest main streets in all Devonshire. Nearly 1½ miles, with a wealth of shops, cafes, and holiday establishments. Early closing is on Wednesday. Combe Martin Bay is beautiful to gaze upon whilst, more practically, there are toilets close by the car-park. Towering cliffs dominate each side of the combe in which the overgrown village nestles. Glance back to the path you have just descended to get the full effect.

Between Combe Martin and Ilfracombe there is a large privately-owned section where rights of way are still under negotiation. For the first three-quarters of a mile you have to stay on the west-bound A399. Continue past Sandaway Caravan Park (or stay for the night if you have a caravan or tent and feel so inclined), and then take the old Coach Road (sign-posted), adjacent to the private drive of Sandy Cove Hotel.

This footpath provides pleasant walking with high level glimpses of the coastline through the trees on the seaward side. The Path rejoins the A399 which must be taken past Watermouth Castle, a 19th century neo-Gothic mansion hall, with a minstrel gallery and a smugglers' tunnel.

About half a mile before reaching Hele, you rejoin a verge path laid by Ilfracombe U.D.C.; this is followed by a short tarmac stretch into Hele itself, with its tiny cove and car park. There are toilets here, a snack bar, and some steep steps which take you up from the cove, around Beacon Point and down into Ilfracombe and its very picturesque harbour. There are some fine high level views of the township on the approach.

4 NORTH DEVON: ILFRACOMBE TO CORNISH BORDER

One of the delights about most West Country coastal towns is the absence of suburbs. Ilfracombe, though large by Devon standards, is no exception. The path begins just west of the town centre and ascends at first towards Torrs Point, and then turns westwards along Torrs Walk. Here is a most scenic and easy grade path, with top level views across the Bristol Channel.

You are quickly on National Trust land, and the next $1\frac{1}{2}$ miles to Lee Bay are along a surfaced road, past Shag Point. The path narrows here, with rugged cliffs to seaward and the golf links inland. A little bit of route confusion around Bull Point; best keep to the higher, inland path if in doubt.

Whilst you can quite easily continue around Morte Point, many walkers, having covered the 4 miles from Ilfracombe, are now ready for some refreshment. If you are amongst them, take the southerly track from the centre of Rockham Bay and follow it into Mortehoe. This is a very historic spot, for the village was supposedly the home of one of Becket's murderers. Morte Point itself, now preserved in perpetuity by the National Trust, was one of Devon's horrors to seafaring men. During one winter alone, there were five shipwrecks on the treacherous headland. An aptly named place, that seems misleadingly tranquil and friendly under the sunshine of a calm day.

Inland, for those seeking accommodation, are a number of caravan and holiday sites. One particularly recommended to the touring fraternity is Twitchen Caravan Park, an old manor house with a number of spacious touring paddocks within the grounds. This has many facilities, including a licensed club-house and swimming pool. The location is half a mile south-east of Mortehoe village.

South-west from Mortehoe the coastal path picks up again

near Castle Rock. One is soon once more on to tarmac, this time making the gradual descent into Woolacombe, with its very pleasant promenade, good car-parking and one of the finest sandy beaches in all Devonshire. If the day is clear, Lundy Island may be spied slumbering on the sky-line. This lonely haunt of sea birds is a granite mass rising 400 feet above sea level and was once a regular hide-out of pirates. Woolacombe is small enough to be cosy and friendly but large enough to have all the usual facilities for the holiday-maker. Both Woolacombe and Mortehoe, incidentally, provide strategic stopping places for those wishing to drive part and walk part of this particular section of the Path.

There is a choice, for the next two miles or so, of following the cliff path or, like many of the locals, walking along the firm, golden sands. The southern end of Morte Bay terminates with another headland, Baggy Point. The walking all along here is good, save for a slight deviation of route from the Point, owing to subsidence. After the Point comes Croyde Bay, a smaller but nonetheless fine version of Woolacombe sand, though likely to be crowded during summer, owing to a number of caravan and holiday parks around Croyde itself. Several footpaths lead from the coast into the village, which is a Devon charmer, with a cluster of thatched cottages and a tinkling stream which runs right through the middle.

Whilst the coastal path now follows the cliff edge faithfully, it is usual to take the road which runs alongside to Iron House. From this point, walk due south, skirting the golf links, and then sharply eastwards into Braunton over Swanpool Bridge, $1\frac{1}{2}$ miles away. On the last part of this section the view gives way to a wide vista over the flat estuary country of Braunton Burrows and Saunton Sands, where the Rivers Taw and Torridge flow in to divide dramatically in front of Instow.

The path breaks here and the traveller must make his way to the start of the next section at Westward Ho! The walker can achieve this by taking the ferry from Instow to Appledore, whilst the driver will have to make his way inland via Barnstaple and Bideford. Pause awhile in Braunton though, for here is a settlement with a history going back some 1500 years. A lovely old church, rich in legend and – beyond the railway – some real old Devon cottages that present a scene unchanged for centuries.

Barnstaple, about 8 miles inland from the coastal path, is a necessary stopping place for those who follow the route by car. This is no hardship, for here is one of the oldest settlements in

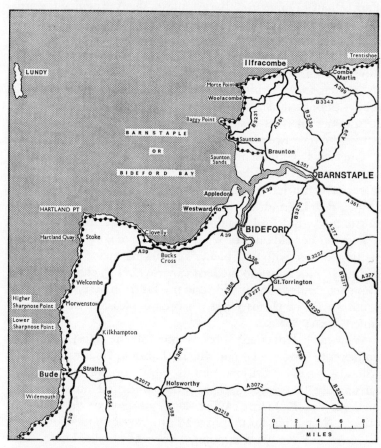

all Britain. Indeed, Barnstaple lays claim to being *the* oldest borough in England. The skyline, as the traveller approaches, is traditional and fair to look upon, only the new civic centre striking a discordant architectural note amid the other mellowed buildings. Most famous landmark of all is the great bridge with its sixteen arches spanning the River Taw.

A richness of history here, where Shakespeare and Pepys

came, and a wealth of old buildings. The modern visitor will welcome the large free car park near the bridge and a comprehensive shopping centre. But the streets are narrow, many of them one-way, and traffic wardens abound in the town centre. There is a convenient touring caravan site at Midland Park, about 1½ miles from Barnstaple on the A361 going towards Braunton, and other kinds of accommodation exist in plenty.

Bideford, too, must be negotiated en-route to Westward Ho! Again this is more of a pleasure than a chore, for this Devonian town is even richer in seafaring history than Barnstaple. As if to emphasise the point, Bideford Bridge has no fewer than 24 arches to Barnstaple's 16. Salmon are netted here in season and in summer there is a slow and constant procession of traffic across the narrow span.

Bideford has a past to stir every patriotic Englishman, and along the quay the fishermen and seamen still gather, as they have for centuries. From this same quay men like Grenville, Drake, Raleigh and Martin Frobisher set sail for the high seas. Fortunately, Bideford has donned her modern mantle without destroying her old one. In what is now a recognised resort, the visiting driver will find plenty of parking space and all the facilities so necessary to modern car travel. The choice of overnight accommodation is wide and not far from here, on the A39 2 miles west of Horns Cross, there is a pleasant caravan site called Steart Farm.

Westward Ho! must possess one of the most romantic names ever conceived – one which, thanks to Charles Kingsley, will always evoke visions of tall ships and adventure. Unfortunately the resort itself is rather dull and uninteresting, modern development having long swallowed the original village. No matter, for there are still romantic connections with Kingsley and Rudyard Kipling, who went to school here. And if the houses are uninspiring, the foreshore does more than make up for man-made mediocrity. Here the great Atlantic breakers come crashing in over superb sands. If, like hundreds of other visitors, you find them irresistible, just hire a surf board and plunge!

The coastal path starts again on the promenade of Westward Ho!, passing lines of beach huts and then an isolated guest house, the last of the town houses. National Trust land is immediately adjacent and the route, an old coastal road, first gradually ascends, then crosses a stile to become a narrowing track heralding the great sweep of Bideford Bay.

The views here are quite marvellous, with the unusual sight of Clovelly nestling in the centre and Hartland Point away in the distance, with Lundy again unmistakable to the north west. The first really difficult part of the Peninsula Path begins some 2½ miles out of Westward Ho! The route is difficult to define and whilst it *is* possible to walk along the beach all the way to Clovelly, this is not recommended; unless you actually enjoy scrambling over interminable boulder-sized pebbles!

Some people do of course, especially beach-combers and shell hunters, but it is not a pleasurable walk. In any case, there is a longish section of undefined way – some ten miles in fact – through private estates hereabouts, so to keep continuity, there is nothing for it but to follow the very stony foreshore at present.

As a worthwhile alternative, and in order to see something of this grand stretch of coast, take the car first to Bucks Mills, a little Devon gem at the bottom of a steep, wooded combe – just a short distance from the A39, signposted from Bucks Cross. Totally unspoiled, it has just a tiny inn, one or two cottages and a store, and some precipitous steps down to the cove. Return to the main road and proceed for about a mile to where you will find a half concealed entrance to Hobby Drive. You pay 4s. for the pleasure of taking your car along this private road, or 4d. if you are walking. Either way it is a route well worth taking to Clovelly, the most famous of all Devon fishing villages. Hobby Drive is open from Easter to October and is without doubt, as one local hedge-cutter described, "most scenical" .Certainly it provides a view of the village from an interesting angle.

Good car parking facilities exist at the top of Clovelly village, but as you will probably appreciate, the whole area is very commercialised. This will not – and should not – deter first timers from exploring this cliff-hanging gem, for it is still possible to see through all the dressing to catch a past-age magic of pirates and pixies.

Clovelly is one of the few remaining places in all Europe which still uses the donkey as everyday transport. There is no option really, for the main street almost falls into the sea down an impossibly steep and cobbled way. That lovely approach road along which you may have just travelled, was given to the nation by Sir Hamlyn Williams and it is an infinitely prettier route than the conventional one. The village itself, not to mention the harbour, might have been conceived and built by an artist, so perfectly do the tiny white cottages, with their creeper and flower-hung walls, blend with the sheer sides of the natural combe. Try to see Clovelly early or late in the season, when the rush is over. Or, if you must take your holiday in August, get there early in the morning. Sunrise and sunset are particularly wonderful experiences in Clovelly, but only if you are sharing them with no more than a few of your fellow men.

Currently, it is hard going on the coastal path from Clovelly westwards to Hartland Point. Much of the route is obscure; it is also heavily undergrowthed in places and there have been a number of cliff falls. Nonetheless, it is walkable for the adventurous. An alternative is to take to the foreshore again, but tedious boulder hopping will be necessary to reach Shipload Bay a mile or so east of Hartland and the lighthouse.

A third method which must be included in this drive-'n'-walk guide, is to take the car from Clovelly car park and along the sign-posted minor road to Hartland Point. Here can be found a large car park and picnic area (charge 1s.), with an interesting 2 mile round-route path, both inland and coastal, via Blagdon and Spright Cliff. Lovely cliff top views stretch in either direction south of Hartland point, the most westerly in all Devonshire and the best from which to see Lundy Island.

Several paths lead from here to Stoke village, which has a most interesting old church and a welcome tea shop. There is a marvellous view point if you take the road from the coastguard cottages towards the sea from Stoke village. Make for Hartland Quay Hotel where there are several car parking places alongside the steeply descending road.

The coastal path may be followed in either direction from here, but the going is somewhat tricky, with much up and down work and difficulty in skirting arable fields. An alternative is to walk adjacent to the official route, by taking the obscure grass-covered lane opposite Stoke Post Office. This meanders south-wards through Elmscott and Hardisworthy (just clusters of farm buildings), and on to an enchanting bay at Welcome Mouth. The distance from Stoke is 5 miles, and whilst this means walking over tarmac, the road is very narrow and cars will be rare indeed. This is a largely secret Devon lane, part of the old coastal road system, deep-set between thick hedges for much of its length, then breasting the open cliff tops and wind-ing down to the sandy cove to pick up the coastal footpath once again.

Just half a mile south of here is Marsland Mouth and the termination of the North Devon section. Whilst this is the man-made county boundary, the walker will notice the distinct scenic difference as Hartland Point is rounded. The cliffs more rugged, the number of villages and hamlets decreasing. The combes and hinterland are not *quite* so luxuriant and cosy. Already Cornwall begins to make its geological influence. There is sterner stuff to come.

Section Notes

The total distance of the Somerset and North Devon coastal footpath is 82 miles.

Bus Services: Lynton to Ilfracombe
Ilfracombe to Barnstaple.
Barnstaple to Bideford.
Bideford to Clovelly.
Clovelly to Bude (Cornwall).

5 NORTH CORNWALL:
MARSLAND MOUTH TO NEWQUAY

Even in a car, most visitors experience a tiny thrill of achievement as that romantic word "Cornwall" looms up at the
county boundary. The very last county in England, a wild and
rugged place where even today, in a society almost entirely
sceptical, tales of pixies, pirates and smugglers are readily
believable. Cornwall is blessed with few of Devon's softer and
kindlier combes, but is nonetheless regal in its barren sternness,
with a coastline that simply couldn't be more majestic.

To cross the boundary line on foot, just above Morwenstow,
is a truly memorable experience, especially if the clouds are
scudding and the white caps are freckling the sea. Stunted
trees, tortured into witches broomsticks from years of yielding
to the relentless westerlies, are proof, if any were needed, that
here is the first land mass the winds have assaulted in three
thousand miles.

This is not easy walking, from Marsland Mouth up on to
Marsland Cliff and on towards Morwenstow. A challenge,
however, to the vigorous, especially if he has stayed awhile to
bathe from the secluded beach at Welcome, on the Devon side
of the border. A lovely little cove this, by the way, known to
few and only accessible by the narrowest lanes.

The cliff path remains rugged for the next 6 miles and much
scrambling in and out of gullies and ravines is necessary. This
stretch is infrequently used and it is not difficult to see why.
There is little in the way of habitation along the coastline from
Clovelly in the north to Bude in the south, and so far there
have been relatively few long-distance walkers. Consequently,
the path is ill-defined in places and often obscured with
bracken. No-one walking this stretch, therefore, would want
to miss Morwenstow, although it lies a little inland from the

actual path. Firstly there is a charming little inn; secondly this is the home of the famous Vicar of Morwenstow, Robert Stephen Hawker, poet and lovable eccentric. The church graveyard here is almost completely filled with the burial places of drowned sailors, many of them laid to rest during Hawker's 40-year term as vicar. His hut, originally constructed from the timbers of wrecked ships, is now preserved by the National Trust and is signposted from Vicarage Cliff. Here it was that he composed much of the poetry that made him famous.

There are a number of paths leading to the village from the cliff route, about half a mile inland. Just over a mile from here, there is an inland diversion, much of it over tarmac lanes, to skirt a disused army camp at Cleave. Whilst this round route is no longer an unavoidable detour it is certainly easier walking than Harscott High Cliff.

Another mile and another diversion. This time around a Services rifle range. Again this is only necessary when firing is in progress, but the inland route is easier. Take the lane north-east from Black Rock, then turn south after half a mile, passing Bethams and Dunsmith. The last $1\frac{1}{2}$ miles into Bude is easy going, thankfully, much of it over level, sheep-cropped sward. The whole of this stretch affords magnificent high-level views of the Atlantic breakers smashing against the granite cliffs. The distance from the Devon boundary to Bude is 10 miles.

Despite being a popular resort, Bude manages to retain much of its mellow dignity. There are beach huts and ice-cream kiosks, of course, but such modern holiday amenities by no means dominate this first resort in Cornwall. Small enough to enable quick orientation, but with a good variety of shops, it has reasonable car-parking facilities and a free open-air swimming pool. Market Day is Friday; early closing day is Thursday.

Bude has an outstanding reputation as a base for surfing enthusiasts. Accommodation ranges from five-star hotels to bed and breakfast houses, with a most pleasantly situated caravan touring park 3 miles to the south, at Widemouth Bay. There are two or three service garages and filling stations at the town's approaches. Bude also has the distinction of being the place where the sea rises higher than anywhere else in the county; bathing other than in the recommended areas is therefore discouraged. The Atlantic surf should never be treated lightly.

If the section above Bude is a little on the rough side in places, that which now follows to Widemouth Sand is a delightful stroll. Leave Bude Centre by the bridge over the scenic old canal, and head for Compass Point. Here are lowish contours, with the path winding alongside a narrow coastal

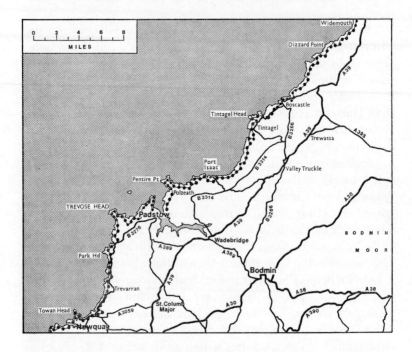

road for about 2¾ miles to Widemouth. When you see the beach, you'll realise why Bude is so popular with surfers; for here is where they flirt with some of the biggest combers in Britain. There is a car park here, and just a sprinkling of houses along the route.

A short stretch of road a mile further on precedes rougher terrain – though no real deterrent to the determined – on the ascent to the heights of Dizzard Point. The cliffs here are really something to see! A fine, gradual descent follows to the tiny cove of Crackington Haven, another surfers' paradise, 10 miles from Bude.

There are two hotels here, together with a car park, petrol filling station, toilets, a drinking water tap – and that's all, except for the bijou cove and minuscule beach. You climb immediately from sea level for about one mile to Cambeak Point and then once more to High Cliff, another 1½ miles further. It is fairly hard going along Beeny Cliff and around Pentargon Cove, but the path becomes more friendly on the final winding descent down to another picture-postcard setting, Boscastle Harbour.

Boscastle is a real little bit of old Cornwall, so enchanting to gaze upon that it deserves the full protection which the National Trust now bestows. The village itself clings to the cliffs sheer above the harbour, but it is the latter that stirs the imagination. A cliff-girt haven in an impossibly rugged coastline, that must have been entered with relief by countless tall ships in the past.

Today there is a free car park with toilets for visitors and the starting-point of one of the premier cliff walks in the entire Peninsula Path route; that between Boscastle Harbour and Tintagel. Marvellous going over springy sheep-cropped turf, flirting with the cliff edges, dipping into ravines, with lovely views inland, seaward, and even downwards at times. About a mile from Boscastle the path skirts Grower Gut, then winds around Firebeacon Hill (what mental pictures that name conjures), past Saddle Rocks and on, hugging the steep and sobering cliff edge. At Bossiney Cove look for the Elephant's Trunk, a natural sea-washed rock formation that is unmistakably like the front end of a pachyderm. Lye Rock is another unmistakable landmark, with The Island and Tintagel Head forming the other arm of the bay about a mile south west. The distance from Boscastle to Tintagel is 4 miles.

Tintagel is renowned for its legendary connections with King Arthur. The headland, with its unique rocky outcrops, rises to nearly 300 feet. Here was the site of a Celtic monastery thought to have been founded at the beginning of the 6th century. King Arthur's Castle was actually built in the 12th century and then lay derelict until Tennyson's poetry began to revive interest in the old legend. So the castle ruins were restored in the mid-19th century. In such a setting no one would wish to destroy the dream entirely; King Arthur *could* have lodged here. It would perhaps be as difficult to disprove as prove. Since legend claims that Arthur lived in the latter part of the 5th century (even before the Celtic monks), why should he not choose this strategic and indeed, regal, headland as his battle headquarters?

Almost more fascinating than the neat, formal Ministry of Works lay-out of the castle ruins is the 14th-century Tintagel Old Post Office. This little gem has a massive slate roof and is laid out inside like a medieval manor house.

The township's main distinctions, apart from Castle and Post Office, are three car-park notices each proclaiming closest proximity to visitor attractions. Needless to say, none is free. There are the usual holiday resort amenities for visitors, with a number of filling stations and a pleasant touring site, called Headland Caravan Park, at the sea end of the main street. Hot showers are available, and there is a nicely kept 3-acre grassy paddock adjacent to cliffs.

Good walking along a well-defined path over lowish cliffs heralds the start of the next section of the route from Tintagel westwards. For about $1\frac{3}{4}$ miles to Port William inlet, the scenery is very attractive and the going easy. Then you have to ascend around Dennis Point, and as the cliffs become steeper the terrains roughen. There is an inland detour from Port William, mostly over metalled lanes via Trebarwith, Trecarne and Treligga hamlets. This was a necessary $1\frac{1}{2}$ mile detour when the coastal area was used as an Admiralty bombing range, but this is no longer in existence. The main coastal path is rejoined above Tregardock Beach.

A pleasant drive along little-used Cornish lanes can be had by leaving Tintagel via the Camelford Road, then turning off to Treknow and Trebarwith. There is an easy bridle path to Trebarwith Strand. The coastal path now skirts a number of arable and grazing farms, near the cliff edges at times and entailing much up and down work. The route is difficult to trace in parts, across open gorse and bracken country. Gull Rock is an impressive outcrop offshore from Dennis Head, particularly if the Atlantic is in one of her capricious moods. More rough walking follows, but the path is clearly defined for the most part on the approach and descent to the lower cliffs at Port Gaverne, 5 miles from Port William. Here the path joins the tarmac road and leads on into Port Isaac, one mile distant. Facilities on the outskirts of the village include toilets and two service garages.

Port Isaac is one of the most beautiful and unspoiled fishing villages in all Cornwall. True, there are a number of new bungalows sprinkling the upper slopes, but these do not detract at all from the harbour itself, which is jealously and rightly preserved. A postage-stamp beach, some dolls-house narrow streets, bright colour-wash walls and an ever-present tang of salt spray combine to create an authentic old-time seafaring atmosphere.

When you can drag yourself away from this little Cornish jewel, take the ascent path past some allotments and then the farmland path to Portquin. Unfortunately for holiday people, there is no right of way along the edge of the cliff, but the inland path traces an almost parallel way for the 2 miles involved and provides fine walking. It stays this way in fact, right around Portquin Bay, passing Doyden Castle (a 19th-century folly) perched on the cliff edge, and some wonderful natural coastal features especially around Carnweather Point. A whole host of thrusting headlands and swooping clefts, with a number of offshore outcrops, delight the eye on the approach to Pentire Point.

It is 3½ miles from Portquin to Pentire Point, the latter now National Trust property. A mile from here one hits the foreshore again, followed by Pentireglaze Haven and the holiday strip to Polzeath, where there is a superb sandy beach, and plenty of stores, refreshment bars and toilets. All kinds of accommodation are available in this area.

For those using Polzeath as a base for the car, the walking from here to Padstow, 3½ miles distant, is interestingly different. The coastal footpath is well defined, first following the cliffs and then descending to the flatter terrain of the River Camel Estuary and the first of the distinctive Cornish sand-dune country; of which plenty more in due course. A ferry plies regularly just west of Rock Quay and the boatman at Padstow is on duty at all reasonable hours, summer and winter alike. Just stand on the beach and wave your arm and he'll row across to fetch you for a very modest charge.

For those unwilling to leave their car on the wrong side of the water, so to speak, there is nothing for it but to drive inland to Wadebridge and then along the southern side of the Camel river. An interesting historical aside about Wadebridge (which drivers may like to recall as they negotiate the fine road bridge), is that during the Civil War, Oliver Cromwell attacked and took this strategic span with no fewer than one thousand five hundred men.

Padstow is another place that retains its essential Cornish charm. It has a pretty quay, a good car park, a couple of service garages, colourful narrow streets and a number of local craft shops displaying surprisingly good quality wares. From this most delightful town, which may well tempt the traveller to linger longer than the itinerary allows, you can walk north-wards along the west side of the Camel estuary to Hawkin's Cove, and thence around Stepper Point to Trevone Bay. Metalled road and a cliff track lead you shortly into Harlyn Bay.

This is yet another sudden delight, especially when approached on foot. A pub, car park and toilets centre on a fine little cove and beach, much appreciated by surfers. There has been a cliff fall just above here, so keep first to the tarmac lane and then the inner footpath, away from the edge, on the way to Mother Ivey's Bay. There is another sea-girt spectacular 2 miles out, called Gulland Rock, with more of the same off Trevose Head; these are The Qules. The path is generally well defined all the way round this headland; the cliffs are now much lower and the scenery inland, with its tamarisk trees and grassy sward, is distinctly Devonian. You can drive out to Trevose Head, but there is a stiffish charge for car-parking. The coastal path skirts a golf links on the south side of the Head, passes the fine sands of Constantine Bay, which sur-prisingly has been left totally natural, and continues to Treyarnon Beach. There is a hotel and a caravan park here – another lovely Cornish coast hideaway, but likely to be popular in the high season. The path continues to Porthcothan Beach and Inlet, where the walking is again on the road for a brief stretch. The distance from Trevose Head to Porthcothan is 3 miles.

More high cliffs now, around Park Head and some truly breathtaking ones in the vicinity of Bedruthan Steps (National Trust). A great tourist attraction, these, not steps at all, but just a natural scattering of rocks below some perpendicular drops. A place to stand and to gaze and to contemplate. Best seen on a wild day when the great Atlantic breakers hurl themselves in full fury at the stubborn "steps". Take care hereabouts, and don't get too curious about the cliff edges, for some of them have well disguised overhangs.

Less than 2 miles to the south, Mawgan Porth adds another sandy bay to the lengthening collection, together with a number of modern facilities including petrol station, pub and caravan park. High cliffs stretch from here to Newquay, and holiday development becomes more and more marked along the approach path round Watergate Bay. There is good walking all the way, though, mostly adjacent to the coast road, with metalled road leading from St Columb Porth into Newquay itself. The distance from Porthcothan to Newquay is 8 miles.

Newquay, which started life as a mere cluster of cottages around a tiny fishing harbour, is now the largest township in Cornwall. It has a new, whiter than white facade which it presents to the visitor; with its modern showrooms, shops, hotels and wide streets it makes no pretence as to its prime purpose. The coastline, the lovely coves and beaches are all there though, despite an almost tangible effort by man to relegate them to the status of an afterthought. A curious thing about Newquay boarding houses, as with almost every other British resort, is that only a sprinkling seem anxious to compliment their county with indigenous names. Thus Balmoral, Cote D'azur and California abound in profusion, but never (or hardly ever), a Trelawney on the swinging boards which grace the villa lines. Wishful thinking perhaps on the part of the proprietors!

Not all of Newquay is new and tourist-conscious, however. The original settlement of "New Kaye" has been in existence since the mid-15th century, when it became a pilchard fishing port and a recognised haunt of some notorious smugglers.

Huer's House, on the distinctive headland, used to be the look-out from which came the signal when fish shoals were sighted out to sea. Good views can be had from the battlements. Other attractions are the Tea Caverns and the old Pilot Gigs in the harbour. Newquay nowadays is recognised as another Mecca of surf-riding in Britain, and the resort claims the finest beaches in all Europe. All the facilities of a large town can be found here, including plentiful evening entertainment.

6 NORTH CORNWALL: NEWQUAY TO LAND'S END

We are now, as has already been mentioned, among Cornwall's sand-dune country and the walk from Newquay to Perranporth is largely through the dune belt. Crossing the Gannel at Newquay, the route is easy and well defined around Pentire Point West, thence to the attractive inlet of Porth Joke. There is a convenient caravan site here, pleasantly located.

The section out to Kelsey Head is also an easy one; then comes the sector around Holywell Bay, a lovely area to admire but with some dunes to cross that are not the easiest on the feet. There is a Services camp on the cliffs near Penhale Point, and whilst it is possible to follow the line of the path along the cliffs and then down on to the foreshore of Perran Beach, permission must be sought before doing so. It is easier, and more pleasant really, to take the inland route from Holywell hamlet, some 3 miles from Newquay. Walk south from Holywell for 2¾ miles, and then along the north-westerly path which leads to the very centre of Penhale Sands. Here can be found the celebrated lost churches of Perranporth. One is thought to be amongst the oldest religious buildings in Great Britain (erected, according to experts, nearly 1500 years ago), and saved from complete burial by the drifting sands during the last century. There is not much to see, but the remains are a powerful magnet to all fascinated by history.

The coastal path now rejoins the beach and continues into Perranporth itself. A lovely name, so Cornish and colourful, yet in fact liable to prove a little disappointing to the first-time visitor who expects a film-set harbour, though the resort is very popular among holiday visitors.

Another well defined stretch of path follows, as the dunes gradually give way once again to solid cliffs. Inland, there is a string of old tin mines – increasing in frequency as St. Agnes is approached and skirted on the seaward side – but the panoramic views along this stretch are marvellous, particularly as you round St Agnes Head, about 5 miles west of Perranporth.

After another 4½ miles of good going over a popular coastal section, you come upon the tiny fishing village and steep cove of Portreath, which offers a car park, some basic facilities and a short road walk as the prelude to another invigorating walk across the Icelandic-sounding Reskajeage Downs. There is some fair going here, along a mainly well marked track, and some grand cliffs below for much of the section – including Hell's Mouth, a satanic maw that should not be studied too long by those affected by vertigo. There are many other deep inlets too, as the path negotiates the cliff edges around Godrevy Point, with its distinctive light-house.

Yet another sand-dune stretch begins here, broken by half a mile of tarmac road into Gwithian, a tiny village with a good touring caravan site (the Atlantic Coast Caravan Park) on the outskirts, adjacent to the dunes and a wonderful three-mile beach of golden sands. The distance from Perranporth to Gwithian is 7 miles. Another church lies buried in the sands of Gwithian, but this time there are no remains to be seen, for although it was uncovered once it has become buried again, probably for all time. The village is approached across a narrow bridge, where wind may well have strewn the sand across the road; the path turns abruptly seawards on the village fringe.

Now follows the 3 mile stretch over dunes, above the most magnificent beach. Indeed, it is possible to scramble down the low earth cliffs on to the billiard-table sands, where the surface is firm and irresistible at low tide. Almost the whole section can be walked thus.

The most direct route to the western side of St Ives Bay is by ferry. This may or may not be in operation; much depends on the time of the year. If it isn't, them turn inland and follow the river bank into Hayle.

Most leisure-bent drivers, searching for unspoiled Cornwall, simply accelerate westwards with all haste at Hayle, which is a pity (or a blessing). For in high summer when St Ives beach is choked, Hayle Sands (which are also Gwithian Sands), remain comparatively empty. Another blessing about Hayle; the food shops give good value for money, with little inflation experienced in summer in more exotic coast resorts. Be this as it may, Hayle is no fun to walk through. Nor is the next $3\frac{1}{2}$ miles into St Ives; although Carbis Bay ($1\frac{1}{4}$ miles from the Hayle Ferry), is a very attractive area of beaches and farms providing touring accommodation. But there is a lot of holiday development along this section (inevitably) all the way into St Ives, the path dogging the railway most of the way.

In some ways it is no bad thing that the approach to St Ives is – for the most part – unkindly to the eye. For this only serves to accentuate the charm of one of the most colourful ports in the British Isles, the home of many artists. It is a veritable labyrinth of steep streets, cobbled passages, archways and old cottages, all diligently preserved and colour-washed in a riot of pastel shades. The artists' studios, shops and little cafes surrounding the clean, sandy harbour with its bouncing fishing boats, create a haven of easy-going serenity. This is one of those rare places where people still have time to stand and stare; at each other, at the sea, at the fascination of their surroundings. When the sun shines there is more than a touch of Italy about St Ives – southern Italy at that.

There is also a matchless white-sand beach alongside the harbour, which the walker or the driver first sees from an elevated viewpoint on the approach road. All in all, St Ives is a Cornish spectacular, to be explored on foot, high season or low. There are a number of car-parks on the outskirts: for your own sake don't spoil any first visit to this idyllic spot by driving into the centre. You *can* do so, but the distractions of local motoring will prevent you from seeing anything at all.

At this stage of the Peninsula Path, we come to the most rugged stretch of all, which only the toughest walkers will wish to tackle. From St Ives to Cape Cornwall, a distance of 16 miles, the route is heavily overgrown (where it is definable at all), and constitutes a long and punishing battle with a tangle of undergrowth. A long, hard haul, well off the beaten track, where accommodation and refreshments will both be in short supply. Not only this, but there are still sections that really are impossible to negotiate. Not surprisingly, for although this will eventually form one of the most exciting lengths of the whole long-distance path, it is at present virtually unused. As implied, the toughest and most determined fell walkers may regard this as no more than a challenge, but for the majority the temporary alternative will almost certainly be favoured.

This entails walking the inland path, which begins three-quarters of a mile west of St Ives, between Higher and Lower Burthallan and continues due west through Trevalgan, Trevega, Tregerthen and into the fascinating little hamlet of Zennor. There is a car park, an inn and a famous church here, of which more in a moment. The path is $3\frac{1}{2}$ miles in length, and winds over high, rough moorland, a landscape of jutting rocks, gorse and bracken. This is North Cornwall at its most severe, wild and windswept; the track was used for hundreds of years by native Cornishmen who thought it prudent to walk half a mile inland from the savage sea and the treacherous cliffs.

Zennor church is a little beauty; square, grey and unobtrusive from the outside, but within a wealth of beautifully proportioned stone arches. And, rare for any church, an atmosphere that is cosy, warm and *homely*. The bell-ringers' ropes hang just inside the door for all to see, and there is the Mermaid of Zennor, a carved bench-end in the small chapel with a legend of tragic allurement. The carving is thought to be over 500 years old. The church was built in 1450 and there is a memorial stone on the outside wall to one John Davey, the last man to speak the traditional Cornish language.

There is a climbing club headquarters not far from Zennor, testimony – if any were needed – to the severity of the coastal cliff faces. From Zennor Church there follows a fine walk to Zennor Head and on, above many craggy inlets, to Gurnard's Head and beyond. Admittedly this is only a short stretch, about $3\frac{1}{2}$ miles, but it is a significant one and well worth tackling. The path is well trodden, no doubt by generations of Zennor inhabitants.

Alas, near Morvah, the route deteriorates again. Whilst it *can* be walked, there is no clear definition of a path from here to Pendeen. Best to take to the road at Rosemergy, walk into and through Morvah, beyond which a good path will be found leading to Portheras Cove and the cliffs, westwards to Pendeen Lighthouse. It is tin mine country now and a fairly marked track leads to Cape Cornwall, albeit an up and down one with some forbidding cliffs, coves and inlets. Cape Cornwall has a coastguard station, a small boat slipway and a hotel. It is a wild and lonely spot, desolate in winter, without doubt, but very attractive in the sunshine.

The working township of St Just is only a short distance inland; this is a town of character with a spacious square (unusual for Cornish coastal towns), and a clock-tower. Quite large too. St Just may take the visitor somewhat by surprise until he reflects on the number of mines in the area. Though some are derelict, many are still working, as the rust-stained sea between the mainland and the treacherous Brisons Rocks offshore will testify. From Pendeen to Cape Cornwall is 3 miles, and from here to St Just, $1\frac{1}{4}$ miles.

You can conveniently rejoin the coastal path at Lower Bosavern, a mile from St Just centre, to stride out towards Land's End 5 miles distant. This is a lovely stretch, at first across lofty cliff tops, then dropping down to the superb sweep of Whitesands Bay, and finally into Sennen Cove via a short step on the road.

Sennen Cove is not exactly a jewel among Cornish harbours – with places like Port Isaac as a yardstick – but it is an honest, purposeful fishing haven which still remains a working village. It has largely resisted the lure of holiday commercialisation and there are some picturesque corners with a harbour wall that invites leaning elbows and sea-gazing reverie. There is a small car park and toilets at Sennen and there is no question that this is the place from which to approach the westernmost point of Britain's mainland.

The Peninsula Path curves around the last bay, giving fine views of the curiously-named Dr Syntax's Head and Longships Lighthouse a mile and half seawards from the point. The cliffs hereabouts are as rugged and noble as any that Cornwall has to offer. From Sennen to Land's End it is but $2\frac{1}{2}$ miles, a short enough distance in itself, but long enough for the walker to feel a pride for these tiny islands and the sea-faring people whose sailing ships bucketed past this point over the centuries, bound for half the world away. A fitting place to end the first leg of this longest of long-distance footpaths.

Section Notes

The total distance of the North Cornwall Coast Path is 121 miles, from the Devon border to Land's End.

BUS SERVICES: Bude to Boscastle and Tintagel, via Camelford and via Wadebridge to Padstow.
Padstow to Newquay
Newquay to Perranporth
Perranporth to St Agnes
St Agnes to Portreath, via Redruth
Portreath to Gwithian and Hayle, via Camborne, and to St Ives via Camborne.
St Ives via Zennor, Morvah, St Just, Sennen, to Land's End (Summer Service only, 8th June to 8th September).

7 SOUTH CORNWALL: LAND'S END TO FALMOUTH

There is no question at all that the finest way to see Land's End is via the Peninsula Path from Sennen Cove. Sadly, much of the promontory has been spoiled by straggling, piece-meal development along the A30 approach road, but happily this man-made ruination makes little impact on those of us arriving on foot.

The distance from Sennen is just 2½ miles, short enough in itself, but long enough for the walker to absorb the dramatic atmosphere of this, Britain's westernmost point. A time to reflect on our seafaring history perhaps and the derring-do of the sea-dogs of long-ago. It is said that anyone who can sail around Britain, with her high tides and dangerous coasts, can sail anywhere. Nowhere is this more apparent than at Land's End, where the Atlantic always seems angry and frustrated as it hurls itself against the massive granite cliffs. A walk, then, between Sennen Cove and Land's End – though the dream will inevitably be shattered at the point itself, try though you may to keep away from the bustle by veering ever nearer the cliff edges via a welter of well worn paths.

Here you will shake yourself philosophically back into the present as you reach the first of the First and Last inns, the shops, houses and hotels, the filling stations and other symbols of modern life. There is a car-park here for a thousand cars, an absolute necessity in the high season, which gives an idea of the through-put of visitors. Trinkets and mementoes are sold by the score, predictable for the most part as to quality, although you can find one or two local stone items worth studying. Here too is the Instant Signpost, where you may add your hometown beneath the words "Land's End" and be photographed in colour. Accommodation of all kinds packs the vicinity of course, from first class hotels to bed and breakfast houses, and there is a well-run touring site called Sea View Caravan Park, situated three-quarters of a mile from the point, alongside end of the A30.

This, then, is the romantic Land's End. Dignified, disdainful, despite all the sophisticated paraphernalia. Blessedly, all the modernity is concentrated into one area, and only a few steps away lies beauty that is natural, majestic and almost timeless. Walk on then, as soon as you can, to explore the shoreline ahead.

Aptly, the start of the southern half of the long Peninsula Path winds across magnificent scenery from Land's End to quaintly-named Mousehole (pronounce it "Mouzel"). A delightful start it is, too, for you can be in the midst of a souvenir-hunting throng one moment and almost totally alone the next. Descend southwards from the Land's End Hotel and simply follow the path of your choice, for there is a whole network of them hereabouts. Significantly, they evaporate to just a couple within half a mile or so. Throughout this route to Mousehole, there is the option of an outer path, which faithfully follows every cliff contour, or an inner one which cuts across most of the headlands. In a mile you skirt the Bay of Nanjizal and some impressive rock faces on the way to Gwennap Head, 3 miles from Land's End. Keep a sharp eye as you approach Porthgwarra Cove, for this is a favourite haunt of seals.

On past St. Levan, where there is a fork path to the hamlet, and the celebrated Minack Cliff Open Air Theatre, where summer plays are staged amongst the rocks. Steps descend to Porthcurno which, on approach, forms a splash of white sand against the contrasting dark cliffs. On close inspection, though, the "sand" will prove to be composed of minutely ground shells. Several Atlantic cables emerge from the sea at this spot.

The route winds upwards again now, and over lovely National Trust land to the unique Logan Rock, some 2½ miles from Gwennap Head. A slight detour is needed from the main path to see it, plus a little bit of easy rock scrambling, but the way is clearly arrowed to the massive 65 ton boulder, teetering on top of a rugged outcrop. So delicate is the balance that it can be rocked by hand. A short path leads from here to Treen hamlet, where there is a pub and a car park. An easy path leads eastwards to Porthguarnon, and then a couple of short detours may be necessary to reach Lamorna Cove. If doubtful, take the inland road via Trevedrain and then, after one mile, turn south-east at Stone Cross, to follow a choice of routes back to the coast.

Lamorna Valley is particularly attractive, a long fertile ravine which descends to Lamorna Cove. A lovely name this and there is no disappointment for the visitor. Just a tiny harbour and slip-way, a refreshment kiosk and a few fishermen's cottages. A profusion of boulders litter the edges of the natural inlet. All the way up Lamorna Valley there are artists' studios, most of them only too pleased to welcome visitors. There is also a grand old pub called "The Wink". It is approximately 4 miles from Logan Rock to Lamorna Cove via the road detour.

There are now 1¾ miles of good walking along the cliff edge, with a final half mile of tarmac on the descent into Mousehole. This place has been described as the perfect Cornish fishing village. A huddle of cosy cottages and a narrow maze of streets cascade down on to the working harbour. A great attraction, inevitably, to the summer throngs and, like St Ives, better seen during spring or autumn, when the fishing nets drape the harbour walls and the little boats are bustling. A short walk takes you to Penlee Point and on to the road to Penzance. It is 3 miles to Penzance centre.

Penzance, a favourite place of Daniel Defoe, is the western terminus of the Cornish Riviera Express and port for the steamers to the Isles of Scilly. Famous for its spring flowers, palm trees and sub-tropical gardens, it has an excellent shopping centre and a balmy, restful atmosphere. Much of this due to its location, tucked away, as it were, around the corner from the wild Atlantic. There is a wide promenade, some good service garages and a large holiday site with touring accommodation at Eastern Green. Penzance is stately and attractive approached from the west, though not so scenic at the eastern end, with its welter of railway sidings and new development. Most of the way to Marazion is built-up, so walk on the foreshore if the tide permits; this is much more pleasant than the road route through Long Rock. When the tide really recedes, you can walk out across the sands to St Michael's Mount; or you can take a boat from the mainland. This unique land-mark, which dominates the seaward view along the whole curve of Mounts Bay, is an old castle and priory, steeped in history dating back to Norman times.

Just past Marazion the coast path veers south-east and follows the lowish but rocky cliffs above Perran Sands. Then inland briefly to skirt Perranuthnoe, and a steady climb upwards and outwards to Cudden Point, with an in-and-out path to Prussia Cove, 7 miles from Penzance. There is a coastguard station and a small beach below Kenneggy Cliff; then, after rocky Hoe Point, comes another holidaymaker's delight, Prah Sands. Here is a mile of silver, at its most scenic when the tide is out, for when the spring tides come there is but a sandy sliver. The beach, the car park and all the usual beach-side facilities combine to provide a good place to pause for a bathe if the day is hot – to refresh yourself for the climb up to Trewavas Head and the 4 miles to Porthleven.

This charming Cornish fishing port, though modern in parts, still retains a strong atmosphere of its seafaring past. The jetty juts out into the sea for a long way, and from it there are fine views back over Mounts Bay and onwards to the Lizard. There are good facilities in the little township.

A mile of road walking leads to another of the rare excursions from the Peninsula Path which must be advocated. The Loe is a two-mile stretch of fresh water forming Cornwall's largest lake, separated from the sea only by the narrow sandbank of Loe Bar. The coastal path crosses this bar, but before pushing on, take the opportunity of visiting Penrose Walks. There is no public right of way, but there is a permissive right for walkers. Open every day except Sunday, these lakeside paths are considered by many to be the most beautiful in the county. Vehicles are not allowed; neither, regrettably, are dogs.

For those exploring the coastal route, more rugged scenery awaits. Return to the Loe Bar then (another sea-bird haven) and proceed on over soft cliffs to Halsferran. There is some subsidence hereabouts, so take to the road briefly for the descent into Church Cove, around the headland from Halsferran Cliff. An alternative inland road cuts out this headland if you prefer. The distance from Porthleven to Poldhu Cove is 4¾ miles.

Poldhu is yet another Cornish delight. Over the little bridge and there it is, just a postage-stamp of silver sand, rocky cliffs

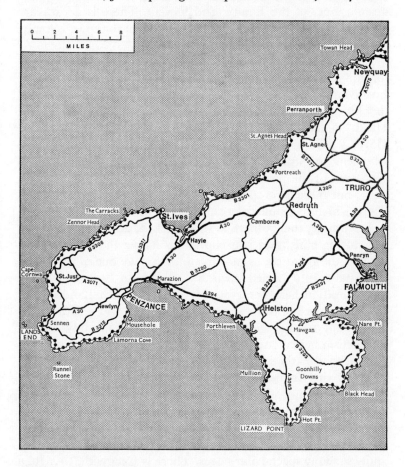

and grassy topped slopes, with white breakers and like as not the sea spume freshening your face. Take the hotel road from here, and then the well-defined path over National Trust land, ascending to the Marconi Monument. This marks the site of the experimental station from which Marconi transmitted the first trans-Atlantic message in 1901.

The path continues above Polurrian Cove, a grand inlet, and down to Porth Mellin, alias Mullion Cove. Here is a fine cavern to explore at low tide when the harbour is dry, and also the impressive Lion Rock. In this area the serpentine rock of the lower half of the Lizard Peninsula begins, replacing the granite faces of the Land's End variety. There is a caravan park at Mullion, and the village, a mile from the cove, is finely preserved and well worth seeing.

A truly wild and majestic stretch of walking now crosses forbidding rocky headlands, magnificent along the shoreline, but contrastingly dull and uninteresting inland, across the desolate Lizard peninsula. The route winds past Predannack Head, Vellan Head and The Horse, and down to Kynance Cove, 4 miles from Mullion Cove. Kynance, with its natural grandeur and strange formations of serpentine rocks, is another high spot of the path. It has a car park and a little souvenir shop, but there is no spoliation, thanks largely to the National Trust which owns much of the land in the immediate area.

From here, the footpath is well marked, despite the ruggedness of the cliffs, and you can either follow the coastal track around the point or, as most people do, take one of the many little paths into Lizard town, 1½ miles from Kynance. Commercialisation here is regrettably on a par with Land's End; there are more of those straggling buildings and a rather flat, windswept terrain with a dearth of trees. Certainly all the magnetism hereabouts is concentrated upon the coastline. The old lifeboat station on the Point represents the southernmost point of the English mainland. The usual tourist attractions are to be found at Lizard town, but amongst the souvenir bric-a-brac there are some rather attractive lighthouse models carved from the rich and distinctive serpentine rock.

Back on the path there is now good walking, although not quite so many spectacular coves. There is Cadgwith, though, a pretty and popular little inlet sporting a pub and a car park. Note the extraordinary cliff formation known as the Devil's Frying Pan. A mile further on is another famous beauty spot, Carleon Cove, and 4 miles from the Lizard lie Kennack Sands. A short stretch of road walking is followed by some up and down work onto and beyond Black Head, and then rugged cliffs dominate the whole of the way to Coverack, $7\frac{1}{2}$ miles from the Lizard. This little fishing village is a totally unspoiled working settlement, with thatched cottages and a lifeboat station where visitors may peep through the open door to see a splendid boat, brasses agleam, straining at the hawser with the eagerness of a rescue dog. For the traveller, there is also a car park, complete with toilets.

After Coverack, there comes a stretch of the path where all but the purists, anxious to maintain continuity, will give their feet a rest and take to the local bus or their car. For whilst it is possible to walk the next 7 miles to Helford, it is tough going for much of the distance; what is more, the path veers off inland after rounding Lowland Point, to by-pass a mile or two of quarry workings on the seaward side. Then there is a near two-mile stretch on the approach to Helford where there is no official right of way as yet and the walker is advised to use the road from Gillan Harbour for a mile and a half. Finally, the coast path crosses Gillan Creek which *can* be waded, but only at low tide. At high tide you have to follow the estuary bank to the hamlet of Carne and make your way by lanes to Helford. However, this whole stretch may be bypassed by taking the bus from Coverack to Manaccan (via St Keverne) and then the ferry from Helford Point to Helford Passage. It is approximately 5 miles from here to Falmouth, and in contrast to the stern cliff scenery behind, there is a perceptible softening of the terrain, with more tree lines nurtured by the river basins of Helford and Falmouth. As you follow the path around the ever-widening Helford Estuary, there is a short restricted section between Toll Point and Rosemullion Head, which entails an inland detour through Mawnan and Rosemullion. Another short road walk is needed at Maen Porth before rounding Pennance Point and passing Swanpool Beach. The actual path rounds Pendennis Point and leads along to the harbour front at Falmouth, but there are more direct routes into the town centre.

Falmouth is a large and bustling seaport, with a big harbour. It is also one of the leading holiday resorts and yachting havens on the south coast of Cornwall. Pendennis Castle, built by Henry VIII, stands sentinel over the entrance to Carrick Roads, a fine natural harbour which shelters all kinds of craft from

61

commercial tankers to minuscule dinghies. This was home to those greyhounds with sails the tea clippers, and the visitor could spend a whole holiday exploring the historic old town and the lovely wooded creeks of the Fal Estuary. Falmouth itself is built on a truly regal promontory, and the views over the town from Castle Hill are marvellous. Indeed, in every direction there are delights for the eye, both natural and man-made.

All the facilities one would expect are here, of course, including caravan and camping sites in the vicinity of Swanpool. Early closing day is Wednesday. After the stern and often sombre coastline of storm-battered cliffs behind him, the walker will appreciate the softer contours, the variety of leafy greens, and the mellow air where sub-tropical flowers grow with ease.

You leave Falmouth, as befits, by water. The little ferry boats ply regularly between Prince of Wales Pier and St Mawes, on the eastern side of Carrick Roads, and not quite so regularly between here and St Anthony in Roseland. These are passenger service only, so car owners may well decide to treat the western and eastern stretches either side of the Fal as separate walks. The drive round the Fal Estuary is complex, running via Penryn, Truro, Tregony and thence southwards to St Mawes – a road journey of some 30 miles.

8 SOUTH CORNWALL: FALMOUTH TO PLYMOUTH

Since the subsidiary ferry from St Mawes to St Anthony in Roseland is somewhat irregular and the service terminates rather early each day (around about tea-time), it is advisable to check timetables beforehand if you intend to walk the next section. Alternatively, if your car is on the eastern side of the Fal Estuary, you can drive down a minor road from Trewithian, through Porthscatho and out to Zone Point. Whether you are walking or driving, however, do not miss this section, for from the end of the promontory there is a superb panoramic view of the estuary and the Cornish coast southwards.

The footpath traces its way around Zone Point, through Porthscatho, where there is a section of road to be walked, and then north-eastwards around Gerrans Bay to Nare Head. It is approximately 9 miles from St Anthony to Portloe. In order to avoid any accidental trespass, take to the inland lane through Sunny Corner, just inland from Manare Point, and follow it into Portloe. From this pretty little hamlet and cove there is a good walk along lowish cliffs all the way round the western side of Veryan Bay. After a short road detour to Porthholland, the path leads on to the attractive cove and beach at Caerhays, 3 miles from Portloe. Gentle wooded slopes flank the bay here, forming a contrast to the open country left behind. There is a refreshment kiosk and a car park on the beach, from which the stately castle of St Michael Caerhays can be glimpsed, lying back from the narrow access road, amid manicured lawns. If it looks vaguely familiar this won't be surprising, for its architect was the designer of Buckingham Palace. The castle is not open to the public.

There are a couple of doubtful sections just east of Caerhays, and it is advisable at present to use the inland road via

Tregavarras and Boswinger. Two routes lead from Hemmick Beach, one via the road to Goran Haven, the other, more attractive, tracing the cliffs around Dodman Point some 2½ miles from Caerhays. The latter is not yet an actual right of way, but as the whole Point is protected by the National Trust, the public have free access. Dodman Point is an impressive headland, a place of treacherous rocks with a massive, 500-year-old tower over 100 feet tall – a familiar landmark to seamen. Goran Haven, as its name intimates, is a refuge for small boats which have made it around "The Dodman" – a snug harbour, a diminutive beach and a pretty little village of narrow and steep streets.

The hills now are friendly, soft-contoured green-caps, and the path winds away around Chapel Point, at first on the metalled road from Goran, to give good walking into Port-mellon. This is a small and very attractive extension of Mevagissey. A nice inn here, called the Rising Sun, overlooks the beach. From here the road must be taken for about half a mile; it is narrow and winding and carries a deal of traffic during summer, so care needed. Mevagissey itself is a colourful and largely old-world fishing village, though there are modern developments, particularly in the Portmellon direction. The streets are exceedingly narrow, with much yellow lining. This is a popular spot with artists and anglers and rightly so; the lovely old town and harbour simply ask to be committed to canvas, while the waters hereabouts are reputedly very fruitful for those with rod and line. The distance by footpath between Dodman Point and Mevagissey is 5 miles.

On over lowish cliffs, a good track leads around Penare Point and down to Pentewan Sands and village. The approach is by a mile of roadside verge which skirts a very popular camping and caravan site, located right on the beach. The sea here takes on a brilliant azure hue, more associated with the South Seas than Cornwall; this is due to the outspill of china clay from inland mines. You'll catch a glimpse of the man-made spill peaks near St Austell, between the green hills to the north west.

There is a quality Cornish pottery at Pentewan, together with essential shops and an inn. From here to Charlestown, an attractive though utilitarian little port serving St Austell, much of the route is along the road from Pentewan, via Trenarran and Porthpean. This last is a pretty little place, with a sailing club, a tiny beach and steep steps to the footpath. From here, it is a pleasant walk by road and track to Charlestown, where the coastal path follows the outer edge of the harbour (no actual right of way, but free access to the public). This point is 6 miles from Mevagissey.

Grazing fields hem the path to Carlyon Bay, a romantic Cornish name conjuring visions of rum and wreckers. In reality, it is a lovely bay sure enough, but filled with a leisure complex established, quite plainly, without concession to the beautiful natural terrain. Crinnis Beach and Shorthorn Beach are two of the attractions here, and there is a golf course adjacent.

Par Sands are next on the route – the centre of the British china clay industry. A road walk of about 1¾ miles is involved, with some necessary deviations from the original path to bypass works expansion. This sector has a desultory fascination, so totally alien is the industrial pocket to the green hills and blue sea beyond the sands. Many caravan sites and associated holiday amenities exist in the area. Leave the road at Polmear, wipe the stubborn clay from your boots, and then push on along the regained coastal path to Polkerris, which is 5½ miles from Charlestown. This section is not yet a legal right of way, but apparently there is no objection to genuine walkers as the well-worn footpath will testify. A sharp drop leads down to Polkerris, little more than a rocky inlet and small beach, but with a pub worth visiting – the Rashleigh Inn. This looks nothing much from the outside, but the mellowed wooden interior is charming.

Some impressive cliffs herald the start of yet another high spot of the Peninsula Path, the section between Polkerris and Fowey. Only 4 miles in length, it takes in the majestic Gribbin Head and then the exhilarating views of Fowey on the western side of the river estuary, with Polruan opposite. It is no penance to walk on the road for the last half-mile or so into this lovely harbour, with its back-drop of luxuriant wooded slopes. A favourite of eminent authors, Fowey has so many treasures that you would need a week to see them all. These include a medieval church, the ruins of a medieval fort, a labyrinth of delightful steep and cobbled streets, and any number of riverside nooks where you become irretrievably drawn to lean and look. Then there is the Tudor house, known as "The Place", and the Rashleigh Mausoleum above the ruined fort. Fowey is fine.

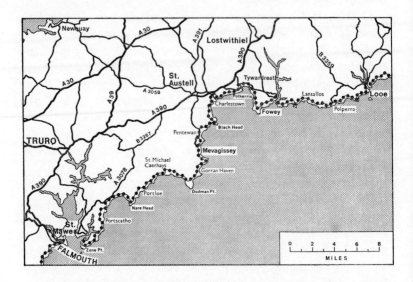

No less enchanting is Polruan, just a 4d. ride on the passenger ferry across the river. Indeed, there are many who find more fascination in Polruan than they do in Polperro. You can take the car across the water here, by the way, but the cost is 4s. 6d. If you think the streets are narrow in Fowey, reserve your exclamations of surprise until you have seen Polruan.

The lovely cliff walk which follows is one that must be approached with reservations. For the experienced walker there will be no problems about the 6½ miles involved, but they could be described as rather tough going, and there are few access points or escape routes once you are committed. Take it on if the spirit is willing, though, for it is a wonderful stretch (especially on a fine day), via Pencarrow Head and

66

Lantivet Bay and down to one of the most famous fishing harbours in the world.

Alas, Polperro has been admired too much and by too many in the opinion of the writer. If you've never seen it before, without its perpetual traffic blockage and trendy dressing, it will still be slightly magical.

Between here and Looe there are numerous caravan sites and other holiday developments, but the coastal path winds serenely on around Talland Bay, where you descend to Talland Cove and nothing man-made save for a small tea shop and a postage-stamp clearing for cars to park. You can swim in seclusion here at most times of the year – a welcome activity after the walk from Polruan. There is more fine walking around Portnadler Bay, with the Looe Island group of rocks enhancing the seaward view. The final mile into Looe is along the coastal road, and the distance from Polperro to Looe is $4\frac{3}{4}$ miles.

Looe is lovely; another tight-knit cluster of bricks and mortar around a natural harbour. The township is divided into East and West by a fine seven arch bridge which spans the river. Possessing strong seafaring and historical connections, Looe is a favourite base for visitors to this part of the West Country.

The Peninsular path rounds the harbour, crosses the 19th-century bridge and zig-zags through East Looe between the sea and the old Barbican. A number of alterations complicate the route east of Looe, and while sections of path exist, they are intermittent. Frankly, it is less confusing to walk along the road for the next 10 miles to Tregantle Down, above Whitesand Bay. An exception is a pretty one-mile stretch between Portwrinkle and the road just south-east of Crafthole. Seaton, 5 miles east of Looe, is a neat but commercialised resort of chalets and holiday amenities with a large car park and a good beach. Seaton blends with Downderry, a largely residential but pleasant enough stretch. Save in the high season the road is not heavily used.

Between Crafthole and Tregantle Down there is a Services firing range, which must be skirted by the road, and on the gradual ascent to Rame Head a rash of holiday chalets mars some superb cliff slopes and fine sandy beaches. Roadside walking is therefore necessary until the final mile to Rame

Head. The distance from Tregantle Down to here is $3\frac{1}{2}$ miles.

From this point there is once more a well-defined path, around the fine promontory via Penlee Point. A short stretch of tarmac follows, through the tiny hamlets of Cawsand and Kingsand; then $2\frac{1}{2}$ miles of lovely path through the parish of Maker, skirting Edgcumbe Park, and on down to the ferry at Cremyll for Plymouth Sound. The great sweep of Devonshire's premier port and city is the final view from the Cornish coastal footpath; if the weather is kindly as you wend your way down from Rame Head, it will be a scene to remember for a long, long time. From Rame Head to Cremyll Ferry, the distance is $4\frac{3}{4}$ miles.

Section Notes

The total distance along the South Cornwall coastal path from Land's End to Plymouth Sound is 147 miles.

Bus Services: Land's End to Penzance.
Penzance to Porthcurno and Logan Rock (via Lamorna).
Penzance to Lizard (via Helston).
Lizard to Falmouth (via Helston).
Falmouth to St Austell (via Truro).
St Austell to Mevagissey or Fowey.
Fowey to St Austell, Lostwithiel, Liskeard and Looe.
Looe to Saltash (via Liskeard).

9   SOUTH DEVON :
PLYMOUTH TO DARTMOUTH

Along with Edinburgh, Plymouth must surely take a prize as one of the most beautiful cities in the British Isles. Plymouth port is the very hub of our maritime history, second only to London through the centuries; its roll of seafaring sons of derring-do is as impressive as any in the whole world. In its time it has also been the greatest naval base in the world, harbouring first the high-sided wooden men-o'-war, and later the mighty ironclads.

Today, there is a gleaming new civic centre to replace war-time devastation; it is of outstanding merit – a tribute to modern architecture. The shopping centre is considered the best in the West.

Old Plymouth is still there, however, represented by the Barbican, where narrow Elizabethan streets and fishing quays still retain an almost tangible aura of the city's illustrious past. It was from here that the *Mayflower* sailed to the New World in 1620 and where Sir Francis Drake calmly finished his game of bowls with the Spanish Armada on the doorstep. Plymouth Hoe must be the most gracious promenade in Britain, with its well-trimmed lawns sloping towards Plymouth Sound. Drake's statue (an exciting piece of sculpture to stir most Englishmen to pride, even today), the fine Naval War Memorial and the resurrected Smeaton Lighthouse, with its old candlesticks. Immediately below the Hoe, ultra-modern but pleasing in design, is a superb open-air swimming pool lined with sun terraces. Plymouth, in fact, is not merely the pride of Devon, it is one of the outstanding sea-ports of the world.

There are very good car-parking facilities for the visitor, especially near the Hoe and other key places of interest. The local bus service is excellent. Market days are on Tuesday, Thursday and Saturday; early closing day is on Wednesday.

Back on the Peninsula Path, on the eastern side of Plymouth Sound, the wild coastline ends – or so it would seem to the walker, for the waters slap so gently against the shore, and the balmy atmosphere induces a feeling of such lazy well-being, that the first Devonian steps will not have the same spring as those induced by the bracing Cornish air. This is probably pure imagination, but it certainly seems true as one leaves the pier from Plymouth's Clovelly Bay and walks along the short stretch of road through Turnchapel. The route wends around Jennycliff Bay where the rocky cliffs are low; inland, Staddon Fort testifies to the maritime past of the city behind. A well defined path leads to Bovisand Bay, a popular week-end haunt for the citizens of Plymouth.

Soon you approach a big Ministry of Defence complex, H.M.S. Cambridge, one of the biggest land-based radio and gunnery establishments in the country. If there is firing in progress, a red flag will be flying at Heybrook Bay some $3\frac{1}{2}$ miles from Clovelly Bay Pier, but the cliff path is negotiable and safe enough. A modest building, The Guest House, faces the beach at Heybrook Bay; this, as the locals will be proud to point out, is where Terance Rattigan wrote "French Without Tears".

Beyond here lies Wembury Bay, and the cliffs begin to become more impressive. The walking is good for some 3 miles to Warren Point and the first of the river crossings on this section, over the River Yealm. Get to the water's edge and clap your hands; if the hour is at all reasonable, the ferry will come for you. If you feel like making an interesting detour, wander inland to Noss Mayo and Newton Ferrers, very picturesque villages on the banks of the Yealm. On the eastern side of the river, the path winds first through woodland, then around Gara Point and along The Warren. A fine coast walk this, which continues from Heybrook Bay to Beacon Hill. The coastal scenery is distinctly Devonian, with steep bracken-carpeted slopes interspersed with sheer cliffs and craggy fissures. From Warren Point to Beacon Hill the distance is $5\frac{1}{4}$ miles.

70

The stretch which follows is private, and it is necessary to take the inland footpath. This runs from Beacon Hill summit to pick up the minor road and lanes to Mothecombe village; thence it leads down to the second river crossing, over the Erme. The mouth of this river drains very considerably at low tide, and if you arrive at the right time you can wade across. Failing this, there is a ford about a mile upstream which can usually be crossed. If neither course is practicable, you have simply to walk a further mile inland to cross the road bridge.

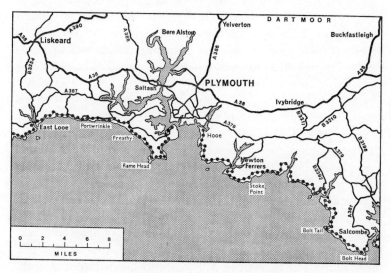

On the eastern side Beacon Point offers seascape views to east and west, followed by good walking round Bigbury Bay, rocky and scenic. There is a clear path to Challaborough, which gives way to tarmac again at Bigbury on Sea, 7 miles from Beacon Hill. Much holiday development is apparent in the immediate area, with caravan parks, mini Go-Karting and a variety of other pursuits. The car park here is large, and there are many yellow lines and "No Waiting" notices. Burgh Island, which can be reached at low tide across the sands, is a lesser version of St. Michael's Mount, with the remains of an old chapel largely overshadowed by a modern holiday building. The sands themselves are good, and this is patently a popular place.

71

The path now follows the River Avon Estuary, *but* – there is no ferry across the river to Bantham since the old boatman has retired. And this one is certainly not wadeable. If you are lucky, you *may* find a small-boat owner willing to give you a nautical lift; if not, it means a long detour inland (some $2\frac{1}{2}$ miles) to Aveton Gifford and the road bridge. From here you can get a local bus back to Bantham, which boasts a post office, a store and a nice little pub. The official path winds around Hams Point and Bantham Sand and the walking is good from here to Thurlestone Sands – a marked contrast to Bigbury is Thurlestone, with a three-star hotel, golf links and limited development. Thurlestone is as sedate as Bigbury is brash. It has good sands, and some foreshore rocks of distinction from which the place name is derived. The red earth of Devon is much more pronounced now as the path crosses a wooden footbridge, passes a second hotel and leads on – with a small section of road walking – seaward of Outer and Inner Hope to Bolt Tail. Take the inner path here, away from the cliff edge, past the coastguard look-out and over National Trust land. The distance from Bigbury to Bolt Tail (assuming you can hitch a boat across the Avon), is $5\frac{3}{4}$ miles.

A truly superb section of path runs from Bolt Tail to Bolt Head, across Bolberry Down, followed by a second section called The Warren (both National Trust). The whole way crosses the tops of some of Devon's most spectacular cliff formations. The descent from Bolt Head down into Salcombe Harbour is one of the coastal path's delights; a scene of heavily wooded slopes, bird's-eye views of the sea and the cluster of Salcombe – that celebrated haven of small-boat sailors.

Salcombe is one of South Devon's most photogenic resorts, with delightful old waterside houses, the ruined castle (which we passed on the way from Bolt Head), a series of fascinating sandy coves and the now familiar, sleepy sub-tropical climate in which palm fronds aren't out of place. To be here for the colourful annual regatta is an experience that all sailing enthusiasts recall with nostalgia. There are good facilities in the town, which has Thursday as its early closing day.

A small ferry crosses from the harbour centre to East Portlemouth; the fee is 6d. The distance to this crossing from Bolt

Tail is 6¾ miles. Once clear of Portlemouth, there is a long stretch of open, wild cliff which continues from Mill Bay right around to Prawle Point, with its isolated setting and rocky foreshore. The path winds behind the signal station, and there is a fingerpost which indicates that Mill Bay is 4 miles behind. It is worth walking inland a mile on from this point, to East Prawle, where there are two inns, a shop – the whole constituting a little Devon coastal hamlet which is much the same today as it was half a century ago.

The path is well defined to Start Point with its famous lighthouse, and just inland, on the heights, the BBC transmitter aerials finger the sky. Superb views can be had from here, some 8¾ miles from Salcombe. You can also look down on the path you will be taking, across Start Bay and all the way to Dartmouth.

In 2½ miles you skirt the hamlet of Hallsands, or what is left of it, for many of the cliff-edge cottages tumbled into the sea years ago. Locals say the cause was extensive dredging of the bay to provide gravel for the building of Devonport Docks. There is a slight deviation of route inland just past here to avoid a more recent land-slip.

Beesands, being at sea level, has not suffered the same fate as Hallsands, There is a caravan site and other holiday development here on a smallish scale, with the forerunner of bigger things to come at Widdicombe Ley. A triangular freshwater lake, this, separated from the sea by a narrow spit of beach. The path runs along this ridge, with fresh water on one side, salt on the other. A dog-leg or two now, to skirt a disused quarry, and then follows the king-sized version of this curious geological feature, Slapton Ley.

Torcross, with its shops, refreshments room and inn, is strategically placed at the beginning of a long straight stretch of road, where you may walk either on the foreshore or on the slightly raised road verge. That long, narrow lake to your left is rich in wild life and a favourite spot for pike fishermen. Slapton sands, a few feet to your right, are among the most popular in Devon, likely to be crowded during the high season.

It is 6 miles from Hallsands to Strete, the first village at the northern end of Slapton Ley, with a long, gradual ascent for

73

the final mile up the old coach road. There is a lovely little cove (but again very popular) on this stretch, called – incongruously – Blackpool Sands. The road continues on through

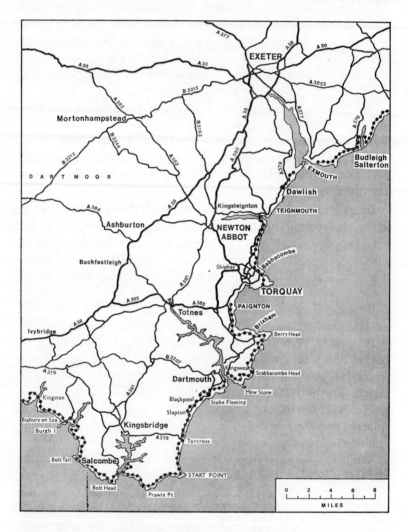

Stoke Fleming, a high-set village some 300 feet above sea-level, with a good variety of shops.

Just north-east of Stoke Fleming, the coastal path forks right and continues eastwards out to Blackstone Point. Very pleasant walking this, for the path is well trodden for the most part around the Point and on to Dartmouth Castle. The distance from Strete to this point is $4\frac{3}{4}$ miles; the section ends hereabouts and you make your own way into Dartmouth, which is about one mile distant.

10 SOUTH DEVON: DARTMOUTH TO DORSET BORDER

Dartmouth is recognised as having one of the most beautiful locations in the country. Certainly the Dart is Devon's loveliest river, and no natural surroundings could outshine the setting for this ancient port – home of Britain's illustrious Royal Naval College.

It could be said, historically, that here is the very cradle of British sea-power. Yet this gateway to the seven seas would be fascinating enough without its naval traditions, for it has a past which can be traced back to Saxon times. Later, it was a great favourite of smugglers. There are very good facilities for the modern visitor, with plenty of accommodation of all types. An annual regatta is held in August. Early closing is on Wednesday. When you have had your fill of this charming port, make for the harbour and the Lower Ferry, which crosses the Dart to Kingswear. The fee is 2d per walker, 2/- for a small car, 2/8d for a large one. From Kingswear, with many a backward glance no doubt at Dartmouth's waterfront, first follow the road which continues to provide lovely views over the estuary. In about one mile from Kingswear northwards (as far as Man Sands) there is a long stretch of coast which has no legal right of way, and detours by road are necessary.

At Crabrock Point the path resumes as an established right of way and winds around St Mary's Bay. A number of holiday camps lie back from the coast between here and Berry Head, but the track is not likely to be crowded at most times of the year. There are wonderful views across to Paignton and beyond as you pass the old fort and then begin the descent to Brixham, another celebrated West Country harbour. Unfortunately, you have to pass a lot of cheek-by-jowl bungalow development on the way down to Brixham. The old middle town and harbour, however, are as delightful as they must have been a century ago. At the Town Quay stands the statue of William of Orange (who first set foot in Britain hereabouts), and hard by is a full-sized sailing replica of Drake's Golden Hind, which certainly adds a splash of Elizabethan colour, even though it is a reconstruction.

It is 3½ miles from Crabrock Point to Brixham. The path begins again half a mile north-west of the harbour, passes the golf links, and terminates again temporarily at Goodrington Sands, 3¼ miles north-west of Brixham. From here the walker must make his own way through the built-up coastal stretch of Paignton and Torquay. Paignton is not at all unpleasant, but Torquay possesses a real elegance. A resort town seemingly conceived, planned and built as an entity, it is a place of wide avenues, green spaces and little, if any, of the garishness one expects to find in a coastal resort of any size.

Tor Bay, for all its pockets of beauty, is not for the serious walker, and although the path begins again just south-east of the centre, near Hope's Nose, it is mostly promenade strolling all the way through Mary Church, past Watcombe Head to Maidencombe. The townside path is fair, but it meanders inland, and only north of Maidencombe does it truly become a coastal path once more. At Labrador Bay it is necessary to follow the A379 before rejoining the cliff-edge route into Shaldon and the banks of the river Teign. There is a ferry which operates from Shaldon to Teignmouth (fee 6d.), or you can walk a little way inland and cross the road bridge. Here there is another break in the path, some 5 miles in length, save for a short stretch on the approach to the River Exe near Dawlish Warren Station.

The reader will therefore appreciate that between Brixham and Exmouth, whilst there are some lovely resorts, the coastal footpath route is mainly over tarmac and is perhaps best covered by car, with occasional forays on foot, for the 20-odd miles involved. The beauty of the red earth cliffs along this coastline, the resorts themselves and the many beaches, should not be under-estimated, however. They are well worth motorised exploration, which could make a welcome change from walking. Make this a driving section then, and give your boots a rest until you have crossed the Exe.

About 3 miles north of Dawlish there is a passenger ferry which crosses the river to Exmouth. Drivers, however, must take their cars northwards to the outskirts of Exeter, and thence via the signposted road south again to Exmouth. The total distance is approximately 20 miles.

The first thing that strikes the traveller who has traversed any length of the Peninsula Path is the level terrain upon which Exmouth is built. It is one of the flattest areas of the whole route. The town itself is a pleasant resort with an historic past that goes back a thousand years to the sacking of the port by the Vikings. Not that there is too much of the past to see, for it is largely swamped by modern development. A celebrated high-spot of Exmouth, apart from the fascinating little harbour, is the Italianate A la Ronde, 1½ miles north of the town. This is an eighteenth century house with an octagonal hall, a shell gallery and other unusual features. Hayes Barton, about 4 miles north-east, is the birth place of Sir Walter Raleigh. There are good all-round facilities in Exmouth; the early closing day is Wednesday.

The footpath starts three-quarters of a mile from the Harbour, opposite Maer Rocks and, passing a coastguard look-out station near Rodney Point, continues into Sandy Bay. The vast holiday camp site here is almost a self-contained town. The path passes through, close to the low cliff edge, and continues past a Services firing range which adjoins the eastern end of the caravan site. There are notices warning walkers that this is not a public footpath and that they are in danger from live ammunition. In this particular instance the military are wrong, for this *is* a legal right of way. However, it would be pointless to argue this with one's dying breath, so if the red flag is flying make a detour, via Gore Lane, inland and on to West Down Farm, where a footpath leads back to the coast.

Wonderful red cliffs now, called The Floors, with the path well defined at all times, lead into and along the sea front of Budleigh Salterton. This is a delightful little resort, just 4 miles from Exmouth, providing excellent bathing in clear water; it has a nice shopping centre and not too much commercialisation. Budleigh beach is famous as the setting of the Millais painting of Raleigh and his friend, as boys, listening wrapt to the old fisherman. Just east of the town the footpath makes a $1\frac{1}{2}$ mile detour around the mouth of the River Otter, continues over a footbridge and heads south again to Otterton Point. From here are $2\frac{1}{2}$ miles of good walking over lowish cliffs to Ladram Bay. This is an inlet of charm, with a car park and touring site, plus a good inn called the Three Rocks – a name taken from the peculiar formations of red sand rocks in the bay.

The footpath passes the inn and starts an ascent which is at first gradual and wooded, but which grows fiercer and more open as it reaches the heights of Peak Hill. This is one of the most spectacular hills in South Devon; magnificent red cliffs, superb vistas and a real sense of achievement as you reach the summit and start the downward rush into Sidmouth. The resort can be seen in fascinating detail long before you reach it.

Sidmouth, like Budleigh and indeed Seaton to come, has a marked restfulness for a seaside resort. Quiet prevails, and whilst visitors are welcomed as enthusiastically as anywhere, this is not done at the expense of the original attraction.

A well trodden bridle path now starts on the eastern side of Sidmouth, leading past the sailing club and ascending some obvious steps. It is $5\frac{1}{2}$ miles from here to Branscombe Mouth, with a couple of inland paths to Salcombe Regis at the 2 mile mark. Worth turning for, this pretty little hamlet, with much Devonshire charm and a pleasant caravan and tenting site at the top of the hill. There was at one time an inland detour at Lower Dunscombe Cliff, but there is now a more direct route, although it snakes across a half mile or so. Keep shorewards, then, from the top of Lower Dunscombe Cliff.

Branscombe beach is a surprise and a delight (save possibly in mid-August when the pebbly foreshore may be crowded). If time permits, do walk inland to the village itself. There is a fine old pub here where you can get an authentic Ploughman's Lunch served on a wooden platter. Set, like the cove, in a deep combe, this is an enchanting part of Branscombe Parish, as is the whole undulating stretch of coastline east of the flats around Exmouth.

The ruddy glow of ochre, so distinctive, so Devonian, gives

way around Beer Head to a cliff formation which is more akin to Dover. Perhaps not quite so white, but chalkily reminiscent for all that. A good path runs all the way along here, with plenty of ups and downs of course. If you feel so inclined, there is an alternative route which winds inland from the bottom of Branscombe East Cliff, over South Down Common and through half a mile of lane into Beer. The cliff path traces its way right around Beer Head, of course, giving superb views

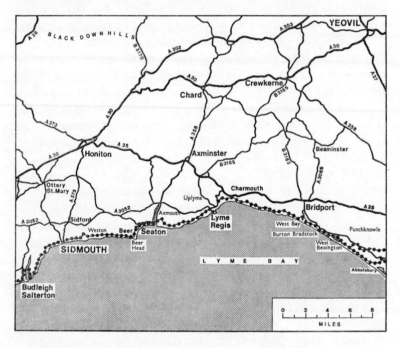

over Seaton Bay. Beer is a nestling village with a past of smugglers and lace-makers, in a setting that easily stirs the imagination. A cluster of cottages at the harbour are dominated by the majestic, towering cliffs, and a haphazard scattering of working boats lie about the pebble beach. Not so long ago a separate and self-contained community, Beer today blends gently with Seaton, some 3 miles from Branscombe Mouth. This is another instantly likeable place, with a quietly pleasing promenade, not too long, and few seaside horrors.

The coast path breaks midway between Beer and Seaton,

continuing east of the latter at first, along the road and over the River Axe via a road bridge. Take the signposted side road to the Golf Course, half a mile east of Seaton bridge, and proceed straight up the first fairway and out via the gate. Don't dawdle, for golf balls can be as lethal as anything ejected from Services' ranges, as the notices will tell you.

The path now enters another intriguing section, the curious Landslip, which entails three to four hours of really rugged walking along a route that is narrow and, in places, heavily undergrowthed. The Landslip is precisely what its name implies – a vast slide of cliff into sea, some five miles in length, which has left a ledge footpath below the original cliff-top contour. Once having entered the section the walker is therefore committed and there is no escape route between the start and the outskirts of Lyme Regis. Only experienced walkers should tackle this stretch – although it must be admitted that hundreds of people do walk it every year. It is way-marked by the local authorities, so if you feel like a little bit of adventure by all means walk on. You will be rewarded with a sense of personal achievement on reaching Lyme.

About half a mile before you reach Lyme Regis, 7 miles from Seaton, you cross the Devon border for the last time and enter a county no less splendid in its own way. Indeed, the Dorset coast path is considered by many to be *the* most invigorating of all in this part of the world. Certainly there are many high spots, as we shall discover shortly. Meanwhile, there is a small change of route at the eastern end of Whitland Cliff. The correct path is the higher one, but the yellow markers will prevent any directional error.

Section Notes

The total distance of the South Devon Path from Plymouth to the Dorset border is 93 miles.

Bus Services. Plymouth to Salcombe.

Salcombe to Dartmouth via Kingsbridge (then ferry to Kingswear). Kingswear to Brixham and Dawlish (via Newton Abbot). Dawlish to Exmouth (via Exeter).

Exmouth to Sidmouth. Sidmouth to Lyme Regis (summer service only).

11 DORSET: LYME REGIS TO STUDLAND AND POOLE HARBOUR

Lyme Regis will be familiar to nearly every traveller who has ever driven westwards along the coastal road; that steep, narrow main street that rises from the Cobb, the Georgian houses and colour-washed cottages, all surrounded by such grand cliff scenery. Lyme has a strong seafaring history, for her ships joined battle with the Spanish Armada, and the ancient Cobb was the landing place of the Duke of Monmouth at the time of the rebellion. Modern shopping facilities are good, but car parking is likely to be difficult in the town itself – though prospects are better on the approach roads atop the hills. Early closing is on Thursday.

To rejoin the coastal path, walk half a mile along the road on the first part of the Timber Hill ascent, then take the footpath which skirts the high-level golf course. There are two paths to choose from here; the inland one is better defined. Lovely walking from here to Charmouth gives a foretaste of the distinctive Dorset coast path to come. There are a couple of short tarmac stretches into the township of Charmouth, which is as picturesque in its way as Lyme Regis. Certainly it possesses good parking facilities for car-owners. Like Lyme it is a very popular summer resort. Not that those who are walking see anything of the township centre unless they detour slightly.

The path winds down to the foreshore and car-park, over the Char footbridge, and then begins the magnificent slow ascent to Golden Cap, the highest point on the south coast of England. Excellent walking, this, for the whole way over a distinctive track; Stonebarrow Hill, a celebrated viewpoint, is passed to seaward. Golden Cap is aptly named, a sand-stone capped bluff which shines in the sunlight and can be seen from as far east as the Hardy Monument (of which more later).

The steep descent from the Cap affords almost aerial views of tiny Seatown with its pub, its one shop, a cluster of cottages and the touring caravan site. This is a delightful little place, with a greensward car park and green cliff-tops as magnificent as anything seen so far. The distance from Lyme Regis to Seatown is 6½ miles.

A series of tempting round-topped undulations occur now on the route from Seatown to Eype's Mouth, via Dog-House Hill, with fine walking, lovely views and a distinctive path all the way. Indeed, the section from Lyme to West Bay, near Bridport, must be included in the top category of Peninsula Path walks. A slight inland deviation must be made about half a mile before you reach West Bay, because of cliff erosion, but you cannot mistake the correct line. West Bay is Bridport's sea outlet, a pleasant little working port which is gradually becoming a leisure resort. The modern facilities here include a municipal caravan and camping ground.

Skirt around the harbour by road, and then start an easy climb, past another golf links, to execute a short dog-leg, below Wennet Hill, around Freshwater Bay. There is a large caravan site here, and dividing paths – the eastern fork leading into Bradstock. The western path is the correct coastal one, which winds back on itself and continues along the foreshore. It is 5¾ miles from Seatown to Burton Bradstock.

An extensive sea-level walk now approaches the famous Chesil Beach, or to give it the correct name, Chesil Bank. At this point, some 3½ miles east of Burton Bradstock, the walker is faced for the first, and only, time with choice of Peninsula Path routes. The main path will be the choice of many purists (especially those tackling the entire length), not only in the interests of continuity, but because here for once is a high level section where the map and compass will have at times to be studied quite closely. Signposting is so scarce that it may be disregarded, though the path itself is clearly mapped. Those wishing to see Chesil Bank in close-up, together with Abbotsbury Swannery and other coastal delights, will press on past West Bexington, the dividing point.

Inland, there is some fine walking, but you will have to thread your way among farms, up and over the roof of Dorset, with the Hardy Monument and the rural route around built-up Weymouth as the attractions. A word of warning, though, to all but really experienced walkers. Self-reliance is needed here, not only to pick the path, but also because this section is 18 miles in length and there is little in the way of habitation for the first twelve of them. Upwey, an extension of Weymouth, is the first place where you will find refreshments and accommodation, and there are five miles more to Osmington village.

If you opt for the high level route, then turn inland from the coast at the Admiralty Underwater Weapons Establishment, West Bexington, and follow the paths up Limekiln Hill, then eastwards across White Hill. The views from here are superb, as indeed they are all the way up to the chimney stack Hardy Monument (this is Nelson's Hardy, not Thomas, though of course we are far from any madding crowd hereabouts!). At present one must follow the road up Portesham Hill as far as the Hardy Monument, but there are hopes of an interesting new alternative route before long. Although the Admiral's memorial is rather dull it is a marvellous land-mark for the walker, and from its base one can look out over Portland Bill to the south, with the path continuing south-eastwards.

The Hardy Country vistas which follow are marred, though not overly, by lines of pylons stretching starkly across the Dorsetshire hills. At the 11-mile mark, join the road southwards for half a mile and then, if you are spartan enough to bypass Upwey, head east for a mile before turning south into Bincombe. This well-preserved Dorset hamlet has a square neat church and a couple of farms, but no facilities. Carry on past the "No Through Road" notice, over Green Hill, West and East Hills and White Horse Hill – where there is a giant chalk cut-out supposedly of King George III, on horseback, wearing a cockade hat. After a mile of descent you reach Osmington village. There are several small caravan sites between here and Osmington Mills, where the coastal path is rejoined. There is a smallish, stony beach here, with a car-park, a pub and toilets grouped in a very pretty little cove.

Instead of the lengthy section just described, however, it is possible at West Bexington to take the coastline path mapped as an alternative to the main route. This will be useful for those

84

who may wish to find accommodation in Abbotsbury or Weymouth. Chesil Bank and the Fleet, like Slapton Ley in Devon, has a miniature advance guard; this one is called Burton Mere. The path runs along the ruler-straight shore to West Bexington and on to turn inland half a mile east of West Fleet Water and Abbotsbury Swannery. Visitors come from all over the world to see this historic bird sanctuary, one of the biggest in Britain, and certainly among the oldest. If you have a dog with you you will not be welcome, for obvious reasons.

The path threads its way through Abbotsbury, a truly ancient and graceful Dorset village of mellow stone and thatched roofs. A monastic centre for centuries, it was also the scene of bloody fighting between Royalists and Roundheads during the Civil War. There is good accommodation here, with inns and a garage. The route here almost circles the unique St Catherine's Chapel, a beautifully preserved hill-top sentinel, solitary and windswept, which dominates the village of Abbotsbury. Currently it is a little difficult to select the correct path east of Abbotsbury, and some detective work with the map may be needed. Some travellers may find it easier to walk on lanes and tracks direct to Langston Herring and thence south to regain the coastal path. Either way there is good walking through a lovely valley, with the high inland route and the Hardy Monument clearly visible. Elm Tree Inn, at Langston Herring, provides accommodation.

The coast path continues past the Moonfleet Hotel, a gracious converted manor house with its own private stretch of the Fleet. From here, the route makes a gentle ascent past a coastguard look-out point, and leads into East Fleet along lowish banks. There are now a number of twists and turns to be made around the natural bays, past a Services firing range at Tidmoor Point, before crossing the ferry bridge at Portland Harbour into Weymouth. The distance from West Bexington to Abbotsbury is 4 miles; from Abbotsbury to Langston Herring, 3 miles and from Langston Herring to Weymouth, $7\frac{3}{4}$ miles.

Weymouth is a very popular seaside resort with all the facilities and entertainment one would expect. The Pavilion holds a particularly good theatre and ballroom and there is accommodation in the town to suit every taste. A large holiday caravan settlement is situated on the outskirts; local attractions include a comprehensive shopping centre, superb sands and safe bathing in shallow water. Early closing is on Wednesday.

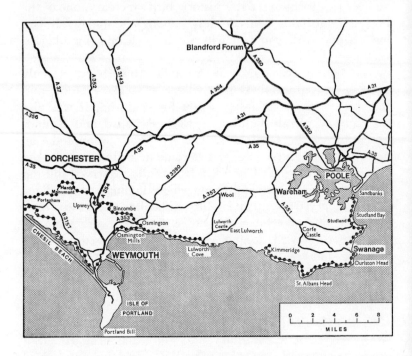

The Peninsula Path recommences one mile east of Weymouth, at the end of the groynes near Overcombe. More fine cliffs begin here, especially at Redcliff Point and Black Head, and continue on the descent to Osmington Mills, where the inland and coastal paths merge. The going all the way from Weymouth is good, and the distance is $3\frac{1}{4}$ miles. From Osmington Mills one proceeds along a well-marked track, at first hugging the low cliff coast and then passing beachwards of a United States Air Force radio station. As one turns inland slightly for the ascent to the superb Ringstead Bay cliffs, the distinctive 'White Nothe' stands out clearly and chalkily.

86

There are two footpaths at the eastern end of the cliffs, with the coastal one threading its way past Bat's Head and Butter Rock. Both lead into one of the most celebrated coves in Great Britain, Lulworth Cove. Wild rocks, magnificent seascapes and a beach surround the ageless rock archway that is Durdle Door. The path is excellent, of course, into the unique Lulworth Cove, a circular bay scooped out of the Dorset downs, virtually hemmed in by cliffs save for a narrow sea inlet. A favourite of the poets John Keats and Rupert Brooke, Lulworth village is a delight to the eye, but don't attempt to see it by car in the high season, for there is hardly any parking space. The area is a magnet for thousands of visitors and there is a caravan and camping ground on the cliff tops nearby. There is also a fossil forest running along half a mile of foreshore, a reminder of the agelessness of these islands of ours. The swimming is good hereabouts, and the area is popular among under-water enthusiasts.

Regrettably, we must take to the car or the local bus now, for the next section of coast is peppered with Ministry of Defence firing ranges. The break ends at Kimmeridge, some 5 miles to the east of Lulworth, and is approached by minor roads. It is possible to cross the ranges by car at most times; if firing is in progress, barriers and sentries will ensure you run into no danger.

Perhaps the best approach is via the breath taking Corfe Castle, then through Church Knowle, Steeple and on to Kimmeridge. In any event it is a lovely drive over the Purbeck Hills, with panoramas that never fail to stir even those already familiar with Dorset. Kimmeridge is a tiny village with a single post-office-cum-shop and a short length of toll road to the foreshore car-park. The charge is 2/6d.

Our path winds up past the 200-year-old folly built, it is said, as a summerhouse for the ladies of Smedmore Manor. If you liked Lulworth, you'll love the next section along the Kimmeridge Ledges to St Alban's (or St Aldhelm's) Head, which must be one of the most dramatic in the country. The path hugs the great fissured cliffs for the 5 miles from Kimmeridge and the seascapes are regal. The track is well trodden all the way with a number of fierce ups and downs,

87

but there are alternative higher level detour paths in a number of places. Chapman's Pool is a jewel, scooped in the shoulder of the Head, as it were, whilst at the tip is St Aldhelm's Chapel. This is a starkly simple stone church, 350 feet above sea level, that has withstood the gales of nearly a thousand years. One can't help noticing the modern coastguard look-out nearby. Itself built to withstand the elements at their wildest, it looks flimsy and terribly temporary by comparison with the Chapel.

The next 4½ miles to Durlston Head contain celebrated high spots where you can stand and stare at East Man, Dancing Ledge, Tilly Whim Caves and Great Globe. One mile from here you reach Peveril Point and move westwards, down into Swanage. Around Durlston there is a perceptible softening of aspect as the land mass of Swanage Bay curves away from the full force of the westerlies. The distance from St Alban's Head to Swanage is 5¾ miles.

The path breaks for the last time on the approaches to Swanage. This is a very picturesque resort, surrounded by white cliffs and sandy bays and located on the so-called 'Isle' of Purbeck. This region of heath, woodland and grassy downs has always been part of the mainland, however, and no-one really knows how the term 'Isle' came into existence. In the past Swanage was an industrious centre for the quarrying of Purbeck stone and there are still many fascinating corners in the old town. The old prison, the 13th century clock tower and some lovely mill-pond cottages are just three of the attractions. Here one can enjoy excellent bathing, skin-diving and sailing, and there are good shops and car parking facilities. Early closing day is Thursday.

The final stretch of the path begins at New Swanage and ascends gently across the Purbeck Hills, via Ballard Cliff, to above the famous Old Harry Rocks at Handfast Point. There is a short stretch of tarmac to be covered through the village of Studland, a charming hamlet with many delightful corners half hidden from the casual visitor, and then only 2¾ miles remain – of gentle, low-level walking close to the lapping waves of Studland Bay – before one reaches the ferry of South Haven Point and Poole Harbour. Across the narrow strip of

In REMEMBRANCE
OF THE FATHER
who,
during more than fifty years,
took Sunday walks
up this combe
with his CHILDREN and GRANDCHILDREN
training them
in the love of NATURE
and of CHRISTIAN POETRY
this
Wind and Weather Hut
was built.

4—NEAR LYNMOUTH

◀ 2—SELWORTHY BEACON
◀ 3—PORLOCK WEIR

5–COUNTY GATE
6–LYNTON

7–THE VALLEY OF THE ROCKS ▶
8–COMBE MARTIN ▶

11—WESTWARD HO!

◀ 9—NEAR WOODY BAY
◀ 10—BARNSTAPLE BRIDGE

12—NEAR WESTWARD HO!

13—BUCKS MILLS
14—CLOVELLY

15—MAIN STREET, CLOVELLY ▶

18–ABOVE BOSSINEY COVE
19–NEAR TINTAGEL

◀ 16–BUDE
◀ 17–BOSCASTLE

20—TINTAGEL
21—PORT ISAAC

22—ZENNOR CHURCH ▶

26—LAND'S END

◀ 23—BEDRUTHAN STEPS
◀ 24—BETWEEN NEWQUAY AND ST IVES
◀ 25—ST IVES

27–LAMORNA COVE

28–MOUSEHOLE ▶
29–ST MICHAEL'S MOUNT ▶

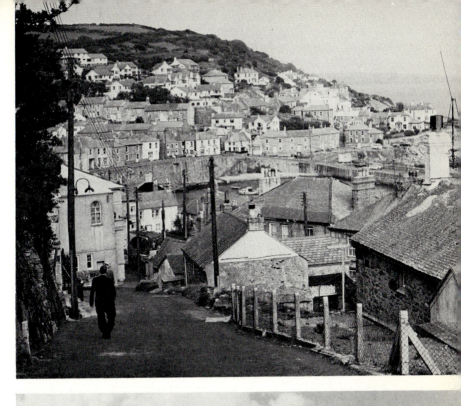

32–HELFORD

30–NEAR THE LIZARD
31–KYNANCE COVE

33—FALMOUTH
34—CARLYON BAY

35—FOWEY ESTUARY ▶
36—POLRUAN

37—POLPERRO

38–PLYMOUTH HOE

39–SLAPTON LEY ▶
40–NEAR SEATON ▶

42–LYME REGIS
43–SEATOWN

◀ 41–BRIXHAM

44-LULWORTH COVE

45-THE KIMMERIDGE LEDGES
46-STUDLAND FERRY

47—CORFE CASTLE

water is the built-up waterfront of Sandbanks, with Poole and Bournemouth in the background.

This is the end of the Peninsula Path, where 4d or 4/- (depending on whether you're walking or driving) is the price of your passport back to the neon and concrete of Bournemouth. You who have walked the whole or parts of this splendid long-distance route, will feel infinitely richer for the experience, having discovered what is still largely a secret Britain to most of her inhabitants.

Section Notes

The total distance of the Dorset coast path is about 72 miles.

Bus Services: Lyme Regis to Weymouth (via Bridport).
Upwey to Weymouth (inland route).
Weymouth to Swanage (via Wareham).
Swanage to Studland (coastal route).
Bridport to Weymouth via West Bay, Burton Bradstock, Swyre, Abbotsbury (summer service only).

NOTES ON THE PLATES

1 Making a start Not all the route is as gentle to the feet as this. Note the sensible use of rucksacks and strong walking shoes.

2 Selworthy Beacon Inscription stone on a hut erected to the memory of Sir Thomas Dyke Acland in 1878.

3 Porlock Weir and the 'Pieces of Eight' coffee house. A good car park and fine walking from here.

4 Near Lynmouth Way-marking is excellent along the Somerset and North Devon section, but you need sharp eyes to spot all the finger-posts.

5 County Gate on the Somerset-Devon boundary.

6 Lynton, together with its twin resort Lynmouth, must be one of the high spots of the whole route.

7 The Valley of the Rocks with car park and refreshment hut in background. Fine seascapes in this area.

8 Combe Martin A well-preserved relic of the more gracious days of travel. The path traces one or two sections of the Old Coach Road.

9 Near Woody Bay The coastline between Lynmouth and Combe Martin has a well-defined footpath and lush scenery.

10 Barnstaple Bridge and some of its sixteen arches. A fine old town with good facilites including large free car parks.

11 Westward Ho! and those celebrated Atlantic breakers. The beaches along this stretch are well worth a visit.

12 Near Westward Ho! En route to Clovelly – easy-going at first but somewhat difficult later.

13 Bucks Mills, a tiny North Devon gem almost falling into the sea. Definitely a place to visit on foot.

14 Clovelly and the near bird's-eye view to be had from Hobby Drive. Note how high and dry the harbour is left at low tide.

15 Main Street, Clovelly One of the few places in Britain where the car is denied access.

16 Bude The canal end at the first resort in North Cornwall. Good walking from here to Widemouth Sands and Crackington Haven.

17 Boscastle and its spectacular little harbour.

18 Above Bossiney Cove A typically dramatic view along this, one of the finest stretches of the path. Note the footpath curling around to the left.

19 Near Tintagel The path undulates with these craggy formations of majestic Cornish cliffs but is well-defined between Boscastle and Tintagel.

20 Tintagel The Old Post Office, a 14th-century building with an interior like a medieval manor house.

21 Port Isaac One of the most picturesque fishing ports in Cornwall with some enchanting narrow streets leading from the harbour.

22 Zennor Church The famous 'Mermaid of Zennor' carved in a bench end reputed to be 500 years old. A fine little church well worth seeing.

23 Bedruthan Steps The Peninsula Path winds right past this spectacular cliff section.

24 Between Newquay and St Ives A typical section of the path in this area. Do not get too curious about the view from the edge.

25 St Ives A view of the harbour. With an almost sub-tropical climate and soft atmosphere, the pace is slow and easy.

26 Land's End is a great tourist attraction, with its massive, stark cliffs rising from a restless sea, and a profound sense of loneliness.

27 Lamorna Cove, an unspoiled beauty spot on a lovely wooded valley.

28 Mousehole The village and harbour; reputed to be one of the prettiest in all Cornwall. Good overnight accommodation and about 3 miles from Penzance.

29 St Michael's Mount You can walk across the sand at low tide.

30 Near the Lizard Incongruous yet fascinating, the Goonhilly Downs G.P.O. satellite tracking station.

31 Kynance Cove, a place of grandeur and strange formations of the serpentine rock. Fine walking over close-cropped greensward.

32 Helford, with its incredibly narrow street. A place of infinite charm surrounded by the wide estuary. A small boat Mecca.

33 Falmouth, the docks and township from Castle Hill. You take the ferry to St Mawes from here.

34 Carlyon Bay not far from St Austell. A lovely bay but how was planning permission granted for this?

35 Fowey estuary A most beautiful part of Cornwall. Polruan in the foreground and Fowey on the far bank.

36 Polruan The main street. You can take the car down to the river level, but it is far nicer to walk. Car parking at the top.

37 Polperro The harbour at low tide. Not many of these boats now fish the Cornish waters for a living.

38 Plymouth Hoe The magnificent statue of Sir Francis Drake. One of the most gracious promenades in the country.

39 Slapton Ley with Start Point in the far distance. The fresh-water lake on the right is a favourite of pike anglers.

40 Near Seaton A typical stretch of Peninsula Path, though it is by no means all as clearly defined as this. When little used the undergrowth encroaches rapidly.

41 Brixham An imposing replica of the Golden Hind, a permanent display in Brixham Harbour. How very *small* these old wooden ships were.

42 Lyme Regis, from the vicinity of The Cobb. Ships sailed from here to fight the Spanish Armada. Difficult car parking in town.

43 Seatown and the little caravan site at the foot of Golden Cap, the highest point in the south of England.

44 Lulworth Cove, most celebrated of Dorset's coastal gems. Almost landlocked, the harbour is a perfect natural shelter. Fine walking all along this stretch.

45 The Kimmeridge Ledges and the approach to St Alban's Head. Some of the finest scenic pathways on the entire route hereabouts.

46 Studland ferry and, opposite, the outskirts of Bournemouth. Some good beaches between Swanage and here.

47 Corfe Castle Though not actually on the route, well worth a small detour from St. Alban's Head. A little bit of preserved medieval England this, the castle and village too.

APPENDIX

TRAVEL TIPS

In an almost unpredictable climate, one can forecast with near certainty that the weather in the South-west Peninsula will be the best in the country, with a high average of sunshine. Perhaps because of this, the area attracts a high proportion of camping and caravanning enthusiasts.

Happily, both groups of independent travellers are extremely well served. Caravan and tenting sites are countless and range from the streamlined mod-con holiday parks, to farm sites providing tranquillity, basic facilities and little else.

Dorset has a very good selection of touring sites along the coastal stretch between Weymouth and Lyme Regis. Charmouth, Seatown, Burton Bradstock and Weymouth itself are all well endowed. Inland between Blandford and Dorchester there are one or two good transit sites for west-bound travellers.

South Devon is a classic touring area with Exmouth, Paignton, Dartmouth and Salcombe all providing high-class coastal sites, whilst inland there are the farm sites amid the wild scenery of Dartmoor.

The northern part of the great western promontory has the big attraction of Somerset with the lovely city of Wells and spectacular Cheddar Gorge, just two of the scenic delights. Plenty of touring facilities hereabouts. The coastline between Watchet and Ilfracombe in Devon, is one of the most visited in the whole country. Blue Anchor Bay, Porlock, Lynton and the rolling panorama of Exmoor makes this area a holiday target for thousands. Notable touring grounds at Blue Anchor and Lynton.

The round tour of Cornwall's coast line is the most popular in the book; and with good reason. The northern route takes in Newquay (a swinging resort with a lot of appeal to the young), a host of touring sites, both tenting and caravanning, and gems like Portreath, St Ives and Land's End. Plenty of farm camping too for those who seek seclusion and are content with basic amenities.

South Cornwall is equally delightful, with Mousehole, Mullion and a hundred other romantically-named coves to discover. Mid Cornwall is perhaps one of the best base-camp areas, with any number of large holiday sites in the St Austell area, from Mevagissey in the south to Looe in the east. If you have to take your annual holiday in the high season, stick to the inland sites if you prefer relative seclusion.

For those who like a solid roof over their heads at night, well, the choice of accommodation is endless. There isn't a village or hamlet that doesn't sport at least one or two bed and break-fast boards and apart from the rush month of August it is almost always possible to find a comfortable bed, congenial company and a generous breakfast to set you off in the right frame of mind each morning.

Of late, there has been a big boom in holiday chalet develop-ment and there is no question that this kind of overnight accommodation is gaining in popularity. Usually as an adjunct to the established caravan site, the chalets are often of the "self-catering" type, giving comfortable quarters but leaving much of the administration to the guests themselves. Charges are thus reasonable and there are some excellent examples, particularly in North and South Devon. The reader will thus gather that any impromptu tour of the Peninsula Path area is eminently practicable at almost any time of the year, without the need for prior booking of accommodation.

Anyone who has toured the West Country will know how easy it is to notch up a surprisingly high mileage in the space of two or three weeks. There are always a number of magnetic places which call for driving detours, and invariably the route will be via winding lanes and hilly terrain.

All of which is a good argument for ensuring that preparation of the car is carried out efficiently. The fact that there are more than enough service and repair garages distributed throughout the Peninsula should be no argument for setting off unprepared.

Routine checking of the car should be automatic, anyway,

and will not be itemised here. Suffice it to say that for hilly terrain the brakes, clutch and tyres should be perfect, especially if the vehicle is heavily loaded or is towing a caravan or trailer. Avoid the heavily laden roof-rack which might make handling difficult on some of those very steep and narrow Cornish lanes. Check your windscreen wipers too, for sudden sea-mists can descend with alarming speed and you will then want every aid to vision available. Finally, do keep a sharp eye for cattle, sheep and farm machinery which may be blocking the lane around the next bend. Often-times you will have very little warning, especially on the back roads that wind close to the coastal footpath. So keep your speed leisurely.

THE LAW AND THE TRAVELLER

by Quentin Edwards, Barrister-at-Law

The South West Peninsula Coast Path is made up of various kinds of highway, as the maps and text in this book show. Roads need no explanation, for we all know them. Bridlepaths may be used by both pedestrians and riders of horses, ponies, donkeys (or mules!) and bicycles. Footpaths may be used by pedestrians only and no wheeled vehicle may be taken on them, except prams.

In law the Coast Path, is, or will be when completed, a public right of way. That description is a complete statement of the user's rights – he has no more and no less. The route is *public*, so any citizen may use it without asking the leave of the owners of the land over which it runs, but his *right* to the route is a right to use it as a *way* only, in other words simply for the purpose of passing along it.

Some of the route runs over or beside open moorland and along cliff tops. Some of it runs through and beside the Exmoor National Park and some of it runs over common land. Nevertheless every foot of its surface belongs to an owner; the roads to local authorities and the paths and bridle roads mostly to private individuals. The only limitation upon their rights as owners is the right of the public to pass along the road or path.

No one walking or riding along the route should forget the owner's position. The name 'National Park' sometimes misleads people into thinking that they are entitled to wander in a National Park as they can in the parks in their home towns. This is not so; the ownership of land in National Parks is precisely the same as elsewhere.

Some of the route runs through, or skirts by, common land. Contrary to popular belief, the public have no right to roam at will across rural commons. The land is so called because various land-owners in the vicinity have rights in common over it – such as the right to graze their sheep on it. Commons should therefore be treated as private property.

As for the sea-shore, there is much ancient law on its ownership and the rights of the public over it. Generally speaking the ownership of the sea-shore and of arms of the sea, such as tidal estuaries, between the mean water marks of high and low tides is vested in the Crown. There are places, however, where the ownership is in the hands of private persons or public authorities. The public have, strictly speaking, no right of passing along the sea-shore except in the exercise of a certain and known right of way. In the ordinary course of things no one ever objects to a person walking along the sea-shore, but it is as well to remember that a right to do so cannot be claimed in all circumstances but only when a path or bridleway runs along the shore.

The wild, rugged shore line along which some of the route runs may also mislead some into thinking that the land about the cliffs and saltings is no one's property. On the contrary, the farmers along the coast make their living from the land just as much as farmers everywhere else, though they may graze the land rather than cultivate it intensively.

All this means that the public who use the route may not roam about as they please in the fields and moors through which it passes. If they do so they are trespassers and liable to be treated as such. Furthermore they are almost certain to do more damage than they realise. Sheep and cattle may be frightened and driven from their proper grazing ground. Although the farmer probably has his working dogs, your dogs will be unfamiliar to the animals so keep them under proper control. Townspeople often do not appreciate that if animals are chased or made to run about they might lose weight (and so value) and, if pregnant, they may abort (at great loss to the farmer).

Summer fields of grass may be a valuable growing crop of hay; grazing trampled and fouled is an asset spoiled; every square yard of a cultivated field is in actual use; farm buildings, though they may be deserted when you see them, are part of a farmer's capital.

Never forget that the land and animals are the farmer's raw material; they are his living and if abused he suffers just as the business man if his factory is broken into or the salesman if his car is put out of action.

As the public are entitled to use the paths to pass along they may legitimately take a reasonable rest when exercising that right. Clearly a walker is entitled to sit by the path and enjoy the view or eat a meal. But camping on the route, except at the places set aside for that purpose, is not lawful. Nor is the lighting of fires or any destruction of the surface of the ground – as by digging a hole for litter. Take the litter with you – after all, you brought it – and put it in the bins which you will find from time to time. If everyone puts a greasy bundle under a stone or in a bush the route will be a loathsome place in a few years.

Some people love to pick flowers, but even on routes as long as South West Peninsula Coast Path this temptation ought to be resisted: if you pick them the rest of us cannot enjoy them. As for the blackberries in the wayside hedges and the cranberries by the path, passers-by have picked them since time immemorial and custom is part of the common law; so pick them in season if you like but be careful not to damage or make openings in the hedges or to stray on to private land.

A great judge has rightly described the law of highways – which is only another name for public rights of way – as the law of give and take. So when you use the Path take only your rights and give the respect fairly due to the rights of your neighbours over whose lands you pass.